Independence Bound

A Mother and Her Autistic Son's
Journey To Adulthood

Independence Bound

A Mother and Her Autistic Son's Journey To Adulthood

A guide for professionals, families, and those persons who associate with adults having autism

---

By
Jacquelyn Altman Marquette

Foreword By
Nancy Dalrymple

Harmony House Publishers

Library of Congress Number 2001095962
ISBN 1-56469-085-7
©2002 Jacquelyn Altman Marquette
First Edition Printed 2002
by Harmony House Publishers
P.O. Box 90 Prospect, KY 40059 USA
(502) 228-2010
Printed in Canada

www.IndependenceBound.com

DEDICATION

For the wonderful gifts of life and love, I dedicate this book to my son Trent who has autism. He has been my greatest teacher in life. I learned to live with hope and gratitude as we journeyed toward independent living. I also dedicate this book to families who live with the challenge of autism and face their dreams.

CONTENTS

ACKNOWLEDGEMENTS

I thank my mother, Joyce Griffin, for her loving and support-ive care for Trent throughout the years. Trent loves his grandmother. During the transition phase of our lives she always welcomed Trent into her home so I could pursue my edu-cation, studies, and the writing of this book. I thank my mother for listening to my woes through the times I felt sorry for myself. I thank her for encouraging me to focus in the moment and to keep going. I thank her for believing enough in me to let Trent live independently especially when it was difficult for her to accept.

I thank my brother, Craig Griffin, for the sharing of his time and care for Trent the many frequent times I called on the spur of the moment and asked for help. I thank Craig for sharing his time with Trent as they listened to music, watched team sports, and laughed. I especially thank Craig for purchasing the house next door so Trent could have his independent living home in a safe supportive neighborhood. I thank Craig and my mother for playing such a major role in Trent's life. Trent's success in accessing independent living was largely supported by their efforts.

I thank my other two sons, Todd and Travis. First, I thank them for accepting the challenges they faced growing up with a brother having autism. I may never really know how difficult it was for them. I thank them for all the times they were called upon to look after Trent, even when they did not want to. I thank each for their unique ways of showing Trent love and affection. I thank them for being Trent's brothers, as Trent always enjoyed their company and loved them. I hope they will be blessed beyond their fondest dreams as they continue to meet life's challenges.

I thank my new husband, Ralph for coming into my life and accepting both Trent and me as a family. He is a special angel in my life. I thank Ralph for accepting my son Trent and his disability of autism. I thank Ralph for listening to my fears, and dreams and above all agreeing to share in my dreams with me. I thank Ralph for helping me see the gift I gave to Trent by letting him live independently, during the past year when I was so terribly afraid. I thank Ralph for encouraging me to complete the writing of this book and seeing how important the message is to others who live and work with individuals having autism. I thank Ralph for his respect for my work in the field of transition and autism.

I thank Jason Williams for accepting the job as Trent's living assistant. I thank him for his patience and gentle care as he helped Trent accept living independently and to overcome many challenging behaviors.

I thank Scott Howard who worked with Trent as a community coach taking Trent to his bowling league, at the YMCA, and introducing Trent to restaurants, shopping centers, and other community settings. I thank Scott for being in Trent's life for nearly eight years, first as Trent's job coach when Trent was in high school, and now his community coach.

I thank Barry Whaley and Troy Klabor from Community Employment as they participated in the Person Centered Planning process with us and assisted supervisors and coworkers to accept Trent at his various jobs.

I thank Dr. Sandra Milnarcik for offering support to Trent and me at a time in our life when family crises appeared.

I thank Nancy Dalrymple for writing the foreword in this

book. She has been a guiding light to me for many years through her published writings and her methods of supporting individuals with autism.

I thank Harmony House for their willingness to undertake this project to its final completion and for their tireless efforts in editing and designing to make this a better book.

I thank Representative Tom Burch for listening to my issues and concerns as I advocated for necessary supports to help Trent and other individuals with disabilities live independently.

I thank Paula Sherlock for advocating for Trent and me through my legal encounters during this critical transition phase. Her support and advocacy was tireless.

I thank Trent's father, for the sometimes confusing, but important lessons we shared as a family. I chose to learn and seek the gifts from those lessons. I thank him for his monetary support in providing a home for our sons and for giving me three wonderful sons.

FOREWORD

Jackie has shared her story in a very personal way in the hopes that other parents will understand the journey toward independent living for their son or daughter with autism better. Her story will also be of help to parents of children with other disabilities. She felt she was prepared, being a professional in the field, to help her son attain the goals she so desired for him and one that he seemed to be moving towards in high school. However, she found that in spite of knowledge, she just didn't have enough and the emotional part of "giving up" her son along with other crises in her life almost prevented her dream for Trent from being realized.

Although the job of making this happen became Jackie's, it also involved a group of people who became the support team for Jackie and Trent. Jackie talks about needing to have a positive mind - set and belief in people and their willingness to help. She is philosophical and practical in her approach. She refused to become mired in her own difficulties, but in the process found ways to protect herself and her family.

As we look at the current situation for children and adults with autism of all ages, we realize how far we have come in the last quarter of a century. But we do become uneasy when we hear about budget cuts and agency cut -backs when we fully realize how little there is for some people. We also know the enormous challenges that many people face today. Adults with autism are often discriminated against in a variety of ways, including the job force and in leisure activities. Their cautiousness and inflexibility can sometimes seem like insurmountable barriers. Their needs can appear to be so great. However, their needs are not so different from those of others. They may require more time, more patience, more planning, and more understanding. They often do not respond well to time or social pressure. Each individual with autism requires a commitment and willingness from those who interact with them to individualize and learn about them. Sometimes people with autism can advocate for themselves, if we listen. Often they need someone to help them.

Quality of life that Jackie talks about in her book means independence. It means choice and growth. It means being comfortable and being accepted. It means being treated as an individual. Jackie wanted this for Trent and never gave up, even when he appeared to be having difficulties. She tried to see things from his perspective. She sought help when she needed it. She never gave up. People who work with individuals with autism will gain an inside perspective of a family's dream and struggles. This insight will help them be better able to provide for people with autism.

The second part of the book addresses many practical ideas for service providers. Parents with children with autism often don't have the opportunity of the natural transition of emerging independence that parents of typically developing children have. Most parents express concern and adjustment problems as their children become young adults and go out into the world. However, they have had practice as their children grew older allowing them more and more freedom and choice. They often have some idea what the challenges might be. For many parents with children with disabilities, and especially autism, one or more parents or some family member has been a facilitator, advocate, and interpreter for the child for years. Extra vigilance has been necessary throughout the child's school years in all aspects of the child's life. There hasn't been much training in how to be a parent of an adult experiencing "independent living" or how to obtain this goal. In fact, the goal of independent living looks different for each individual and family situation. Hopefully, the young adult has learned to be an advocate along the way or will learn to advocate as he becomes increasingly sure of himself in a variety of settings.

Parents all have hopes and dreams for their children. These have to constantly be adjusted as the child's individual talents and skills become apparent. This is an emerging process. Parents of children with disabilities are often so caught up in the daily life of the child that they may not have had much time to even articulate what these dreams and hopes might be or adjust their original thoughts about this. Jackie states that she had the dream of "independent living" for Trent for many years. However, she hadn't realized how difficult realizing that dream would be for everyone. Her story suggests that we need to consider ways to help families go through the "transition" in a more gradual and natural way as the child is growing up. Each step toward independence and self advocacy - including choice will help. Certainly having a broader range of options for adults and preparing families throughout the secondary school years for the transition are vital.

Throughout these crises years for Jackie and Trent, several life changes occurred at once for Jackie's family. Families have many demands on their personal and financial resources. The larger circle in her community and family helped her through this difficult time. She had to learn to make some significant personal changes in the way she approached her life and what was happening to her. She describes this well. Her story makes us well aware that families need help from people they can trust. At some times they need more help than others. As families leave mandated school services behind the challenge of finding or creating opportunities often becomes overwhelming. This family's story makes all of us realize how much more needs to be done throughout the school and adult years to provide meaningful supports and services for individuals and their families with disabilities and how reaching the goal of "independent living" really means understanding the interdependence of us all.

Nancy J.Dalrymple, Autism Consultant

INTRODUCTION

This book is about my son, Trent, who has autism, the crises we faced during the transition to adulthood, and steps we made together to establish his independence into his own home. Trent's transition to adulthood was a significant time in his life. Transition is defined as the passage from high school to employment or other major life goals such as independent living (Suomi, Ruble, & Dalrymple (1992).

It has been necessary to provide Trent with a high degree of supports and assistance so that he had independent living. Some persons may believe Trent has not actually achieved independence. A definition of independence by Ed Roberts, a leader in the disability movement, claimed that persons with disabilities have necessary supports and assistance in order to live independently. Independence is the control people with disabilities have over their own lives. He further suggested that independence should not be measured by the tasks one performs without assistance but by the quality of one's life with adequate support (Shapiro, 1993). Trent's quality of life significantly increased because of the supports that made independent living possible.

Facing the change during the transition process was fearful for Trent as well as for me. Some of the fears and crises we faced after Trent graduated from high school are:

Fear of....

- Facing Trent's lack of quality in the day
- Costs of supports for Trent
- Relationship changes with spouse
- Losing the support of a loved one
- Ending a relationship/divorce
- Unemployment
- Changing jobs to manage the support needed for your child
- Change within the family structure
- Finding time to advocate for the services needed for your child
- Finding adult programs
- Finding caring and supportive persons who will associate and train the adult young adult.

The transition from school to adulthood is most challenging for every individual with developmental disabilities. Autism is a complex disability, which made Trent's transition form high school to adulthood increasingly difficult. According the Advocate, a newsletter published by Autism Society of America, autism is a:

* complex developmental disability that is a result of a neuro-logical disorder that affects the functioning of the brain. The associated behaviors resulting from autism significantly impacts an individual's social interaction and communication skills. The disorder makes it hard for individuals to communicate and relate to the outside world.

Who Can Benefit From This Book

If you have a family member with autism or a developmental disability approaching adulthood you are probably wondering what your family life will look like after high school is over. You may have a family member with autism who has completed high school and needs help to become more independent. You may be an educator, or an assistant who works with individuals or their families having autism. You may want to know how to further help the person who has autism to become less dependent on others so independent living is reachable.

One cannot discuss the process of transition after high school for the individual without including the family. Educators or adult agency representatives may be searching for strategies to offer families who live with autism and are entering the transition phase. I have described the problems our family faced and the solutions I found that helped us make independent living a reality for Trent and me.

As a parent you may be seeking services or ways to help your young adult become more self - determined. I do not profess to know all the answers. I only offer the steps that led us to independent living. The learning continues for Trent and me as we continue the evolving process. I hope you will find the book to be helpful in understanding how autism and transition affects the individual and the family. Strategies I offer may help you begin the process of planning for your family and your child after high school ends.

How Is This Book Helpful?
This book may be helpful in several ways:
A. To families
    1. I tell our family's personal story to offer hope to families seeking ways to hold their family together during family crises and transition.
    2. I offer perspectives and strategies that helped us cope and maintain hope while I moved my family and Trent through the transition years.
    3. I provide practical steps I used to face the transition years and ways I began to move forward to reach the goal of independent living.
B. To families and those who associate with adults having autism in the community

1. I illustrate strategies that helped build Trent's self- determination that prepared him for independent living.
C. For educators, professionals and policy makers who provide services to families and adults with autism, or who develop community programs
   1. I found gaps exist in the understanding of professionals and policymakers regarding the extent families need support during transition phases. I share our story because it is also important that policymakers know the struggles and the needs of families and persons with autism facing adult years. I want key officials to know that persons with autism are capable of living independently as long as supports are in place. Funding for supports is the critical key to independent living success.

The result of our experiences may be helpful to other families living through the transition years. The families who best relate to my family's situation are those who have a family member with autism requiring special supports in order to live independently or participate in the community. Trent needs significant attention because the effects of his autism are limited expressive language and limited ability to adapt to change.
The strategies and examples presented in the book are general strategies recommended. They are general positive approaches for individuals having autism. The strategies may also apply to other persons with autism both within the home and community settings.

Content of This Book

The book is divided into these sections: Part (1) Struggles to Solutions, Part (2) Expect to Grieve, Part (3) Steps to Designing the Independent Living Arrangement, and Part (4) Trent's message to us regarding general strategies that supported him in learning to live independently.

In Part 1 I offer insights about our movement through the transition process and steps we took to eventually establish an independent living arrangement. Certain strategies are listed that helped Trent and me manage our lives in times of crises, which eventually led me to a new perspective. The perspective helped us move away from our old way of life and into a completely new life. I have also described the basic steps we took to design an independent living arrangement.

I have written Part 2 to describe our personal stories that helped me recognize the grief I experienced because of Trent's transition and our family crises. My uncertainty and confusion about the unknown enabled me to experience and move through the grief process to accept big changes. I learned a great deal by moving forward in spite of the unknown future.

Part 3 and Part 4 of the book presents practical strategies. In Part 3 Designing An Independent Living Arrangement, I offer practical tips about how I found ways to make Trent's independent living arrangement our reality. I also describe the ways I managed my life through the transition phase and moved forward to the new discoveries into independent living. In Part 4 Trent's Message, I provide general strategies that helped Trent adapt to new people and situations. The strategies facilitated Trent's adaptation to independent living and certainly have application to other adults with autism. I share personal examples how others can relate and communicate with Trent as they support him in his new life. The strategies were an important enhancement of Trent's success as he faced new situations, and new people.

Because of the autism, Trent's limited ability with expressive language prevented him from expressing his needs to others. I believed the best way to convey Trent's needs to others was by writing Part 4 as viewed from Trent's eyes. I wanted a brief concise format to fully explain his particular needs for those who might be working with him. It is not practical to assume that every one who associated with Trent would agree to read a book focused on theory and practice with autism. First, it was my hope that Trent would be the one to reap the benefits of having others understand him as they worked and lived with him. Second, I believed persons who supported Trent in the community needed this information to better understand his needs. Third, I wanted Trent's support team to have genuine feelings for his needs, how he responds to his environment, and activities he enjoys.

Planning and Beginning

I have planned along with family members and other support persons an independent life for Trent, by carefully analyzing his needs, interests and capabilities. We are in a continuous process of carving that life for Trent through Person - Centered Planning approach (explained later). Although Trent cannot fully express his future desires to us, we have helped Trent advocate for himself by designing his life to include environmental and people supports that will enhance his success at his job, other community settings, and within his home.

Trent began to demonstrate problem behaviors soon after he graduated from high school that indicated he was confused and insecure about his new life. Trent received funding from a supported living grant. Throughout the past two years, I used the funds to hire several community coaches to help connect Trent to the community, work on decreasing negative behaviors, and strategies that increased his independence.

During the past three years Trent has had five different community coaches. Each has introduced Trent to various environments within the community. David, a middle school teacher, spent Saturday afternoons taking Trent to either bowling, hiking, or to community festivals. Heather was Trent's community coach and introduced him to the YMCA. She was also my best friend's daughter and has been close to our family for years. Scott who recently became Trent's community coach had been Trent's job coach for the last few years in high school. Jason currently lives with Trent and has been a roommate and community coach to him for over a year.

Roommate, Jason

Community Coach, Scott

For the past six months Jason and Trent have been working together in a large retail store. Jason was hired at the same time as Trent, to provide Trent with the support he needed in order to learn and keep his job. Each one of Trent's support persons has enriched his life by offering various cultural, intellectual, and emotional guidance.

Developing Perspectives

Through much turmoil and confusion I have learned to develop a perspective(s) toward my life that pulled me through the turbulent times. Some of the perspective(s)s involved the following:

First, I had to learn to accept that I simply do the best I can each day for Trent and me as I earnestly progress toward the goal of independent living. Second, I learned to accept the crises in our lives. During those difficult times I learned it was OK to put my needs first and take care of myself if I were to become fully capable of attending to Trent's needs. Third, I learned to let go of a specific outcome I had expected while pursuing independent living with Trent. I began to open my mind to new people, new opportunities, no matter how frightening. With this new attitude, I began to see doors opening up for Trent and me. I believed that having hope regardless of the bleak outlook and trusting in a higher power to guide me through the crises and fears sustained me.

My Benefit in Writing This Book

I gained a sense of peace knowing that this book provided input to those who associated with Trent during those times I was absent. The transition years of leading up to my letting go of Trent were some of the most unsettling and insecure times of my life. Letting go of Trent and trusting him to others was a most frightening and difficult experience for me.

As I mentioned before, I wrote Part 4 so others who worked with Trent would understand how to help him. The more I thought about how my writing served the purpose of helping others support Trent, the more I ironically felt empowered to let Trent live independently. I assured that I was empowered in two ways: (1) the book was my way of advocating for Trent indirectly and, (2) my direct participation was through communicating frequently with Trent's support team.

I began to eventually trust in the 'letting go' process and recognized that with choosing independent living, I realized the gift I was giving to Trent. Through my letting go of Trent, he had the opportunity to embrace his life and grow as an individual. He began to learn about himself and the results of his choices without total reliance on me. He still continues to face changes and obstacles daily while having the supports from others. He also has the opportunity to choose to belong in a world that at one time excluded persons having autism. The ultimate goal was for Trent to learn ways to adapt to change and enjoy his new independent life without relying totally on his family.

My hope also is that this book will reach out and become just one small tool that may serve the purpose of helping others understand what families living with autism endure. As others recognize and understand the issues that families living with autism face, these realizations become the first step toward making independent living an achievable goal for adults who have autism.

Who Is Trent?

Trent is 24 years old and has autism. But autism is only a small part of who Trent is. He has a distinct personality and characteristics that make him personable to others. 'Affectionate and gentle' are often the words that come to my mind when describing Trent. His teachers once called him a 'gentle giant'. He enjoys belonging to a group, even though he has significant weaknesses in socializing. He reveals through his behaviors that he wants to belong, be accepted, and supported. Trent thrives on his routine. A routine helps him make sense of his environment and the time of events. He has learned to become more independent with help from others and by building into his routine these specific tasks:

- caring for his body (showering),
- listening to his CDs,
- assisting in house work and preparing dinner, washing and drying his clothes.

Community activities such as: grocery shopping, running errands, and participating in recreational activities with his roommate, community coach, and family have also become a vital part of Trent's routine.

Trent's favorite past time is going to movies. Eddie Murphy and Jim Carey have been his favorite actors. When he grocery shops, Trent enjoys purchasing the items needed on a weekly basis or for special celebrations. His memory is very good when it comes to choosing regular weekly items such as orange juice and milk. Other favorite activities include walking his dog Bumper, riding his bike, walking in the park, bowling with his community coach, and eating out in restaurants.

Music is therapeutic for Trent. Not a day goes by without Trent listening to music. He loves to slow dance, sing along to songs on the radio, and listen to piano music. He enjoys all kinds of music especially classical. Music fills our home.

Trent loves his brothers and exhibits smiles when they come to visit. His brothers play semi-rough with him. He enjoys the physical contact. Trent shows strong affections to members of his family through big bear hugs.

Trent enjoys taking his day slowly. It is easy for me to appreciate the way he approaches certain tasks. He has an incredible attention for detail. For example, he enjoys assisting others when preparing dinner. He shows facial expressions of delight, as he chops fresh vegetables or works on other kitchen tasks. He enjoys every step of the cooking task, as he works very meticulously and slowly.

Trent's attention for detail at times drives me crazy. For instance, he has had a ritual of turning lights off and closing doors before he leaves home. I believe he does these rituals because it provides him closure and assists with his transition to the next activity.

Trent is often calm in ways that I strive to be. I sometimes rush through my day and overlook the small parts of life that he enjoys so much. I take life a lot slower whenever I watch Trent move slowly through the steps of an activity (i.e. cooking). Whenever I slow down in order to stay at his pace, the waiting has a calming effect on me. It becomes therapeutic for me whenever I practice taking delight in the small steps of an activity or task as he chooses. There are other occasions when I recognize he must keep up with us. We are both learning.

Trent has had several opportunities for work. As Trent worked at his jobs, he smiled, walked with a spring, and even socialized with coworkers by singing with them to songs on the radio. Work was not always problem - free for Trent. He has had several jobs ranging from the grocery store, retail store to food services. He has lost several jobs due to his extreme need for others to understand his disability. For example, Trent had a job at the YMCA working in the laundry and he was terminated after a couple of months. Twice Trent became agitated or confused when his routine changed. Trent needed his employer and coworkers to understand how to help him as they introduced him to work tasks and provided a supportive routine.

It was not easy to find an employer who agreed to be open to providing the supports Trent needed. For example, strategies for supporting Trent included a flexible undemanding work schedule, consistent routine, and a safe place to withdraw when he became too overwhelmed by his environment. His job success was dependent on others providing these specific supports in the work place. As these supports were provided, Trent performed his duties and in turn his employer gained a reliable and valuable employee.

Trent has had some difficult years with the transition from high school to his new adult life. He has had to live through several family crises and his parents divorced. Feeling unsure about how he would fit into his new life was extremely unsettling. The changes were fast and furious rather than slow and easy as he would have preferred.

Part One

STRUGGLES TO SOLUTIONS

T rent was three years old, when I first found information about an agency that successfully placed adults with autism in community environments. Community Services for Autistic Adults and Children (CSAAC) in Rockville, Maryland provided residential and community living programs. At that time I knew very little about adult options. I assumed that by the time he was an adult it would be easy to access an independent living program. As Trent approached adulthood, his goal was to have a natural home and to live a typical life of leisure and work that the rest of us enjoy.

In reality, that goal was not easy to achieve.

Family Crises

The monumental task of carving independent living into Trent's life was solely my responsibility. I often felt discouraged and saddened during the transition process as I worked toward Trent's independent living goal. My life became even more complicated as I struggled to plan and arrange Trent's life in the midst of several major devastating life events.

I was faced with the challenges of separation, divorce, financial loss, unemployment, and my youngest son, Travis' cancer. I chose to withdraw from my work during these difficult times and became temporarily unemployed in order to rest. I needed time to sort through my issues in order to understand what was happening to me and how I was going to handle it all.

Perspectives Learned
from Crises

Experiences from my obstacles and struggles offered me a better perspective. The insights I learned were meaningful. I discovered techniques that helped pull Trent and me through difficult experiences. I want to share with you the insights I learned that led me to progress in the transition years as both Trent and I adapted and grew. By sharing our experiences with other families, you the reader may begin to see that options are possible for your adult with autism and your family.

Surviving

I learned that at times the goal for Trent and me was merely to survive the moment. I now realize that it was OK to feel this way and that sometimes there were times that just surviving was the best I could give. But I found through the perspectives there were ways Trent and I could eventually thrive. I learned that having hope was the answer to thriving that pulled us through the crises. My perspectives did not occur overnight. They came slowly as Trent and I faced obstacles and lived through the struggles.

How The
Perspectives Helped

I became more receptive to this new way of life, and that led me to consider options and to choose new priorities I had never once considered. I began to diffuse for the first time some emotional strain from our lives when I accepted a new openness. Trent and I found safety among new opportunities and supports as we entered into the unknown and faced the crises. I gained insight from the struggles that led me to a new perspective. This new perspective helped connect Trent to his new way of life in adulthood.

Can Other Families Find Independent Living?

Yes indeed. Trent has independent living. Each family living with autism has a dynamic function and relationship that makes the unit unique. Our crises and situation may or may not be similar to other families. I believe that similar perspectives are needed when families face the transition phase and as they accomplish tasks to reach independent living for a family member. At times it seemed impossible to first let Trent go to living on his own and second, to find the supports to make it happen. Other families can also sustain and find ways to make the dream of independent living come true, too. Independent living was reachable for Trent and it can be reachable for other families as well.

Adult Agencies

Trent lives independently, without an agency's support. I am responsible for hiring, training, and financing the arrangement. Trent's name is on the State's Medicaid waiting list. There are very few agencies in our state offering independent living. Either Trent and I had to wait for years, or I had to find a solution.

It has been my experience in working with agencies as an educator and as parent seeking services for more severely involved person with autism, that many agency representatives believe their difficulties are too great to train the individual. Agencies, such as supported employment vendors, often overlook individuals with autism when considering eligible clients to serve in competitive employment. However, research has shown that people with autism often make very qualified employees. Persons with autism can maintain a job when appropriate supports and a good job match are determined and tailored to meet the individual's interest and disability needs (Smith, Belcher, & Juhrs, 1995).

Individuals with autism are underrepresented and considered by adult services such as supported employment agencies

3

to be "too disabled" to work (Smith, Belcher & Juhrs, 1995). Many professionals still do not understand how to support individuals with autism. Families experience disappointment and confusion when their son or daughter is denied services, because they often do not understand that adult agencies are not required to accept all individuals who apply for services. There is a great need to provide training to agencies so they can better deliver services to individuals with autism.

Necessary Supports

Because of Trent's limited expressive communication, he required a visual support to help him understand a new situation. For example, a written checklist indicating to Trent where he would go and what he would do helped him understand what was expected. This strategy enhanced his success. Although Trent spoke using single words and short phrases, he was always capable of participating in various environments when the necessary supports such as a checklist was offered.

Certain supports such as the checklist enabled Trent to achieve a higher level of success. Without supports, he would not have had opportunities to participate in the community. These supports were critical to Trent's success as he participated in his jobs with other employees and various leisure events and activities that most us are privileged to enjoy.

How was Trent supported? The environments in which I placed Trent required two components for his adaptation to the setting:

1. A job coach or a community coach to develop natural supports
2. The understanding of Trent's needs by others and their willingness to learn how to communicate and to relate with him. Supports and other interventions were necessary in order that Trent adapt to new people and to new environments.

Accepting change was and is still difficult for Trent. When change in the environment occurred before Trent was prepared, he became confused and either refused to participate, or worse, exhibited unacceptable behaviors. Some unacceptable behaviors were obsessing on categorizing or organizing, yelling out, or ripping his shirt. Supports were always and will always be critical to Trent's success and adaptation to community participation. Yet, the supports came with an expense.

Limited Financial Resources

Due to my limited financial resources, I had no choice but to rely on creative ways to arrange independent living for Trent. The Medicaid Supports for Community Living is a federal and state program that provides funding for an agency to provide an array of services for an individual to live in the community. The waiting list was extremely long for those interested in independent living and the only individuals being drawn from the list were those with emergency needs. Trent's number on the waiting list was #699 for the state. I examined my options and realized that if I waited for his number to come up or wait for Kentucky to allocate additional funding, Trent could be waiting years.

I became aware of the importance for Trent to live in an independent living home as early as possible after high school ended. According to research, the most serious problems with respect to community and programs access appeared to be for families who have kept their adult children at home beyond the age that most young adults typically left to reside in the community (Hayden, Spicer, Depaepe, & Chelberg, 1992).

Dr. Lorna Wing (2001) discussed the importance of offering residential services to adults with autism. It has been rare that adults with autism participate in community environments. It may work fine for the individual to continue to live at home after high school if the individual has activities outside the home

5

to participate. The only options often available for the individual has been sheltered environments that offer services in employment and leisure. If no activities outside the home are available for the adult, the individual often becomes engaged in increased repetitive activities. A number of adults tend to dominate the life of the family with the repetitive obsessive behaviors. The longer the behaviors occur the person may become less interested in leaving the home.

A solution for the individual with autism and the family is an appropriate residential service that offers community participation and activities. After high school ended, I began to see Trent's repetitive behaviors worsen. My choice was not to keep Trent at home just to wait for services. I recognized that I needed to develop a new attitude toward considering various options regarding changes Trent, our family, and I would have to make, no matter how uncomfortable those changes were.

Sweeping Changes

Soon after Trent's graduation, I faced the significant challenge of hiring a community coach, providing and arranging activities with others so Trent's days could be filled with some quality. That summer Trent had the job he worked at in high school. The job was working in produce at a grocery store for two days a week several hours each day. But that left a substantial time in his day. It was important to me that Trent experience purpose in his immediate daily life. I felt an urgent need to build quality in his day and to work daily toward meeting the future goal of independent living. I soon realized that family crises were headed our way and my struggles would increase substantially.

Soon after, Trent' graduated, our family crises began. When it came to living day by day with Trent and his adult needs and living through the family crises, I became less functional, and increasingly exhausted. I withdrew from my work, made several major changes in our lives, and set short and long-term prior-

6

ities so that independent living would become Trent's reality.

It was difficult at that time to see the positive effect or insight from our crises. It was much later that I acquired the proper perspective to pull Trent and me through. Our family crises included divorce, financial loss, Travis' surgery and intensive chemotherapy for cancer. When Travis, Trent, and I moved across town, Trent's dependency and his obsessive behaviors worsened.

As an educator, and consultant in a work transition program, I once thought I was prepared to handle the transition years. I have heard that doctors cannot treat themselves. I thought I could apply principles in transition without difficulty, but I was apparently fooling myself.

One of our crises happened with a community coach I hired to work with Trent. I discovered much too late that one of the five community coaches I had hired for Trent had previously served time in prison. I found additional disturbing information about him when a policeman I knew ran a police check on him. I was shocked because when I hired him, his references were excellent and I was relieved that he worked so well with Trent. I had to let him go. Other people were recognizing negative characteristics that I failed to see.

Even today I want to believe Trent was not harmed in any way and I want to believe that the coach's worse behavior around Trent was just laziness. I will never know the truth because of Trent's limited ability to express his needs and feelings.

One might wonder how I as a mother and an educator could have allowed this to happen? I believe I was so overwhelmed with our family crises that I was grateful to have someone available to follow through on community activities (i.e. leisure and employment). I became blind to some obvious clues regarding his character. I was in the denial stage. Since that time I have made a personal policy to never hire an individual to work with Trent without conducting a police check.

All the crises combined were more than I could endure

7

within a two- year period. Life seemed to have handed me new events and tough situations all at once. I was going through major transitions at the same time Trent went through his transition into adulthood. I often questioned why Trent and I had to endure transitions at the same time. It eventually became clear to me how strongly each member of our family was affected by Trent's transition into adulthood and that led to each family member having transitions and crises of their own to handle.

During the crises, I often questioned, "Will there ever be a good life for Trent, our family, and me?" Is Trent capable of surviving our crises? Am I capable of surviving the crises? Will Trent ever be capable of adapting and accepting changes in his future? Will Trent be capable of moving forward in life with the interventions that have helped to build his self-determined behavior? Will Trent ever obtain independent living and have people who are good for him that understand his needs?

The new perspectives that took me so long to develop actually brought me to the very solutions that opened doors so Trent would accept becoming more independent. The effects of all our crises combined could have been detrimental for both Trent and me. But now I realize that the crises made me stronger and surprisingly made Trent stronger.

The new way of life was driven by my dream for Trent to reach his goal for independent living. The perspective I have developed was essential for Trent's goal, yet it was only part of the solution. Trent also had shared responsibility toward reaching the independent living goal. That is, he had to put forth effort, however so small, in accepting daily interventions that helped build his self-determined behavior. All factors combined, pulled Trent and me through our crises.

Transition and Person - Centered Planning

As Trent entered adulthood, I had the monumental task, apart from other families who have nondisabled children, to develop a future for Trent by deciding what work he will do, who will provide support, and where he will live in his new independent adult life.

Working through the process is called transition. A tool to help a family work through this process is the team approach called person -centered planning. Person - centered planning involved team members such as educators, professionals, friends, and extended family members who helped Trent and me explore options and supports before and during the transition process. The process guides the team through activities that helps the individual with a disability express his or her desired future. The process then examines the supports and responsibilities that may help move the individual toward that future (Mount, 1988). We used the person - centered planning approach to determine Trent's path to independent living.

The transition phase is a process that families go through to come to terms with a new situation. The new situation for Trent was to establish a quality of life through seeking independent living that included work and leisure activities after he finished high school.

It was essential that transition occur in order that Trent's past and our family's previous way of functioning disappeared, then our new life became the reality. First, Trent and I had to decide what kind of new life we desired. We then asked what was the ultimate goal? Once we decided the goal, planning occurred, and we set short-term goals so we could eventually reach the ultimate goal. If the change was going to work for Trent and our family, transition had to occur.

I found the process of transition paradoxical. Transition did not begin with the outcome, but the ending of our old situation. For example, after high school, Trent had to inwardly let go of a familiar, comfortable, structured routine, peers he saw daily, daily work and activities that he was used to doing, and a support staff he relied on. Sadly, after high school graduation most of his network of relationships came to an end.

When high school ended, that started the transition phase for both our family and Trent. As Trent and our family started the transition phase, all members in the family had to let go of our old reality and our old identity.

The letting go process was not easy for any of us. I discovered in our family's situation that not all of us agreed to let go of the old. Trent's father who I will call Mike, was not ready to accept letting go of the way our family once functioned. Trent and I needed him to be more available for us. Mike, traveled every day of the week for work. Mike refused the opportunity to make a change in his work that would free him up more to help us. He could not accept the change and most importantly, the new commitment. Mike could not accept the new life so he chose to withdraw from our family.

Letting Go of the Old Life

After graduation, a piece of Trent's world was lost and never expected to return. Facing life after graduation was a devastating time for Trent and our family because we were not prepared.

In order to move forward, Trent had to let go of something (i.e. a network of people who he depended on) and our family also had to let go of our old way of functioning. Transition is the letting go. The letting go was very difficult for each of us to do.

When the old way was eventually behind us, and the new way had not emerged and was still uncomfortable our family operated in what is referred to as the transition phase. The transition phase was the stage between finding our new life after ending the old life. For example, after Trent graduated from high school, the external changes happened quickly for both of us. Inwardly the transition happened much more slowly for Trent and me. To move forward, our family had to let go of our old reality and as well as our previous identity.

Saying Goodbye to the Old Life

It was important that Trent to accept the part of his life that was over. Some of the parts that were over:

- getting up regularly and taking the bus to school
- the individuals that he would not see anymore on a regular basis
- the structure of each school day
- absence of his father in the home

Trent at Graduation

So how did we say goodbye? We created actions and activities that dramatized the ending events. It was my belief prior to graduation that Trent would celebrate the ending of high school as most other students. I arranged for Trent to attend his prom, participate in graduation, and we gave him a party in his honor. In fact, he has scrapbooks of pictures and momentos of these major life events.

We offered Trent a chance to appreciate the memories of his high school years by allowing Trent to take a piece of the old way with him when school ended. The graduation events associated with leaving high school act as an emotional time for all students especially students with disabilities. These events were peak experiences for Trent. They set the stage for his new life and gave him the opportunity to say goodbye to his old life. It was the next phase that proved to be most difficult and fearful for Trent and me.

Surviving in the Transitional Phase

I discovered once I gave myself permission to let go of my previous existence and as I helped Trent let go of his past routines, we both experienced some relief. We were uncertain about what was ahead. Our new life did not magically appear. We were trying new things and waiting independent living to appear in our life. I recognized that independent living would take tremendous work. I saw the transitional phase as the 'nowhere between two 'some where'(s).

Trent's Understanding of His New Life

I discovered that it was not enough for me to understand and plan what was going on in Trent's new life. Trent needed to understand and have his own say about his new world. First, that meant he needed additional supports and interventions that would facilitate his understanding of his new world. Second, after accepting the supports, Trent needed to become active in choosing and applying the supports that would assist him in moving toward independence.

I had to find a way to define for Trent both the past life and the new life that was forming. His understanding of this transition was essential for acceptance of his new way of life. Trent needed to be frequently reminded what parts of his life that were over and what parts of his life that were a new beginning. When Trent learned a new job task, or learned to use the exercise equipment at the YMCA among other members, he worked on new challenges that were initially overwhelming to him. It was important that he had a clearer understanding of his responses to situations and how those responses fit into a new pattern in his life.

I used photos, social stories, and daily checklists to show Trent how new activities and new people can replace parts of his old life. The tools helped Trent come to terms with his new life. Through various communication supports, Trent began to understand the distinction between the old that is behind us and the new that is ahead of us. Trent began to show signs of accepting his new life.

The Old and New Merge

After graduation, the changes in his life were immediate. Trent and I both felt the emptiness and loss as we searched for a way to build a new life. I knew I had to find pieces of his old life that would continue to be a constant support for Trent.

I felt that if I pointed out to Trent that some aspects from his old life would be a continuation into his new life, he would possibly see how he was still connected to the past and his confusion toward the new experiences in his life might decrease. That was the case with Trent. As I showed Trent how others who were still involved in his life and the old familiar activities were still part of his new life, I hoped that Trent would possibly have an increased sense of comfort and security. Here were some examples of the people or activities that continued on for Trent after graduation:

- peers in bible study class.
- walking his dog Bumper in the park daily.
- regularly assisting Grandma and Mom in preparing a favorite dish in the kitchen.
- assisting others with gardening or caring for plants, flowers, or yard work.
- grocery shopping.
- eating Sunday dinners at family gatherings.
- going out to favorite movies or to a favorite restaurant.
- spending time with brothers and extended family.

I reminded Trent regularly that the familiar activities within his day that were to continue. He seemed to exhibit a sense of security knowing that he could rely on certain people and activities. I reminded Trent how his old life was still part of his new life even in the midst of new and experiences.

Facing New Beginnings

I learned a lot about new beginnings. Beginnings are strange and fearful times for anyone. The beginnings were also scary for Trent, his brothers, and me. Beginnings represented a time to make a new commitment and to become the new person and the new family that the new situation demanded.

First, I believe our beginnings established once and for all that our ending was real. Soon after graduation, Trent sat on our sofa lacking the desire to even leave the house or even listen to his favorite music. It was obvious to me that Trent was mourning the end of his old life (i.e. the structured school environment). The two years after graduation, Trent saw fewer people on a day - by - day basis. This decreased his opportunity to socialize.

Second, the new way of doing things represented a gamble for Trent and me. There was always the possibility our new activities and strategies would not work. Immediately after Trent's graduation, I hired a young man to be Trent's community coach. The new person needed time to get to understand Trent and strategies for relating with him. Trent also needed time to get to know his new community coach.

Todd, Trent and Travis

At first, Trent refused to accept the new community coach in his daily life. There were obstacles, and I had to make myself available for training the community coach and to resolve issues. The community coach facilitated the new idea and a new routine for Trent. The new way I planned on often seemed unrealistic to me because Trent did not want to accept his new activities and the new community coach. I learned as Trent and I forged ahead with unfamiliar and uncomfortable stages we were at the same time learning and growing. Thus, we were making progress.

Third, I believed our new beginning might trigger old memories of failures that negatively affected us. I'll always remember those particular times during his school years when Trent experienced great difficulty in adapting to changes, and exhibiting inappropriate behaviors. I was on call to Trent's teachers as we all

worked together to design consistent plans. I suppose I remembered those particular times because they were so difficult and I was terrified of revisiting those same old familiar issues.

During Trent's high school years, he had a place to belong, and daily work sites to learn tasks. He exhibited a comfortable self - esteem. He had nondisabled peers in the high school choir who were his buddies and friends. He had favorite teachers he relied on because he was secure knowing he could depend on them. They were his social connections. After school ended, he had no stable social connections except for a bible study class on Sunday mornings. Losing those stable connections triggered in him a sense of loneliness and possibly personal failure. This led to Trent's setback after school ended.

I thought I was fully prepared to accept Trent's new beginnings. As a special educator and a student in research, I studied many aspects of transition while I earned degrees. Living right in the middle of the transition phase as a real participant, I quickly discovered that with my struggles, my perspective was entirely different from the perspective of the 'experts' who at a distance wrote scholarly material on transition theories and strategies.

I realized I was really living all the technical jargan that the experts described in books on theory about families in transition. I resented the writing, and I thought that they left out so much about how families live. I once considered myself prepared to handle Trent's needs for transition into adulthood. Due to the divorce, I was left on my own to find coping strategies to handle the needs of Trent and or family. I suppose there was no way to really prepare for the crises but to live through it, and recognize coping dilemmas. Big changes were headed my way and I was afraid.

Change

As I was browsing through cards at a gift shop one day, I found the following description of the meaning of 'change'.

Change Means

> C hances to Grow
> H opeful Beginnings
> A dventure to take
> N ew paths to follow
> G reat opportunities
> E xciting new places

It's meaning was simple and basic and offered me hope for the dream I held of independent living for Trent. I became hopeful for a brighter future for Trent and myself. The process of change may be viewed with a perspective that moves us forward in our lives and relationships.

Change Was Inevitable

Change comes whether we're ready for it or not. I began to believe, that I might as well welcome change as opposed to fighting change because change was heading my way. My new - found way of accepting the changes was much easier to say than to do. It took me some time to practice it and to develop it into a habit. I experienced suffering and joys through change. I discovered how important it was to open myself up and accept my circumstances no matter how bad or how bleak. I intuitively knew that if I was going to get through my circumstances I had to let go and accept any possible outcome, even if the outcome was negative. This perspective moved Trent and me forward into our new life. This perspective helped us move from the previous surviving stage to the thriving stage of our new life.

Out of desperation I held onto openness and acceptance and released trying to control details to survive. I was handling my situation as best as I could and that is the only thing I knew. I noticed the focus educationally and politically of advocacy groups have been toward increased funds for families and their disabled members. Professionals who developed programs for individuals with disabilities focused their efforts toward seeking additional funding to either maintain already developed programs or modify those programs to improve services. Those efforts are needed.

However, what is missing from the picture are ways that funding can trickle down to provide direct support for families and the disabled family member. Families need help with ways to advocate for their child with autism and acquire supports and services. Families also need help to acquire a perspective to get through the transition years so that the family adapts into their new life as well as the individual.

Funding does open doors to services for our young adults. I discovered without the small funding offered to Trent his community opportunities would not have unfolded. I also discovered funding wasn't the total solution to forming Trent's new life. I had to find ways to cope and accept our circumstances during the transition phase in order that I become open to new ideas that would help Trent enter into his new life.

If I had chosen to remain closed about the future, I do not believe Trent and I would have the independent life style we have now. Without an opened attitude my fears may have prevented me from taking leaps through the doors that were opening for Trent and me.

Trent had no program after he graduated. He had a small state funding stream that paid for a community coach for a few hours a week. A community coach was hired to provide Trent with various community opportunities in different settings. Only a small part of Trent's needs were met through the service of a community coach. In order to increase quality in other areas of Trent's life I was left to carve his community involvement within my own network of contacts:

- family,
- friends, and the
- community connections or events.

I had to set short range goals in order to reach the ultimate goal of independent living. The short-range goal included hiring a community coach but also acquiring community inclusion using a network of family and friends however so small. I recognized I was fortunate I had some extended family supports that helped Trent and me get through the transitional phase. I recognize in retrospect how important it is for planning to occur long before graduation. The entire family would eventually have to change to accommodate the needs of Trent.

Accept Change - Questions to Consider

I developed questions to consider during the planning stage. If I had known the questions earlier before Trent graduated, I may have been better prepared when the changes happened fast and the crises occurred. I wished I had these questions available to ponder before the planning for Trent started. These questions were critical in order for all of us to adapt during the transition and crises phase.

Plans should be made effectively, in order to necessarily project years ahead. Consider these questions. They may help your family begin to face the inevitable changes and new beginnings:

About your adult child's stability of the day
- After high school what is actually going to change for my family?
- After high school what is actually going to change for my son or daughter?
- How can we carve a stable day for our child?
- How will our child know stability in his day?

About your child's routines of the day
- What will be my child's routine of each day?
- What familiar persons will he associate with?
- How will his day or week be structured?

What are the secondary changes that your change will probably cause for your young adult? for your family?
- Will a family member be required to leave his/her job or change the hour at the job?
- Will someone need to be hired in the home and supervise the adult for a short time?
- Will a community coach need to be hired to provide community recreation activities?
- Where will I look for a community coach?
- Have preparations been made in order to transport the individual to job site or day habilitation center?

What are the further changes that those secondary changes will cause for the individual? for the family?
- If the individual has a community coach transporting him/her to the job site, what training will need to take place so the community coach can meet the goal for teaching skills for independent living?

Family members will have to let a part of their old life go.
Who is going to have to let something go?
- Will the family member need to take time away from a job to plan, prepare, and follow-up with job coach or community coach hired?
- Have plans been developed on specific independent living skills on which to work?
- Will the individual with a disability have to let a familiar daily routine go?
- After high school what is over for everyone in the family including the individual with autism?
- Is a comfortable routine over with for the family?
- What ways can the family compensate for the previous routine?

How well are we managing the endings of our old lives? I have provided a basic checklist that assists a family in developing a perspective that will help pull a family through the changes and through the difficult times.

A Checklist

Developing A Family Perspective
How To Manage Endings

1. Have I estimated my family's change carefully and identified who is likely to lose what-including what I am likely to lose?
   ____Yes   ____No

2. Do I understand the subjective realities of these losses to my family members who experience them even when they seem like they are overreacting?
   ____Yes   ____No

3. Have I acknowledged these losses with sympathy?
   ____Yes   ____No

4. Have I permitted my family members including our child with autism to grieve?
   ____Yes   ____No

5. Have I expressed my own sense of loss?
   ____Yes   ____No

6. Have I defined clearly what is over for my family, my son or daughter, and for me?
   ____Yes   ____No

7. Have I defined clearly what is not over and what is the same for my family, my son/daughter, and myself?

____Yes ____No

8. Have I found ways to "mark the ending" for our child and for our family?

____Yes ____No

9. Am I being careful not to denigrate the past but, when possible, to find ways to honor it?

____Yes ____No

10. Have I made a plan for giving my family and each family member piece of the past to take with them?

____Yes ____No

11. Have I made it clear how the ending we are making is necessary to protect the family or conditions on which our family depends?

____Yes ____No

Part Two

EXPECT TO GRIEVE

"He who lacks time to mourn, lacks time to mend" is a quote by William Shakespeare. I think William Shakespeare was right that if we are going to cope with our unique family situations, we must offer ourselves time to mourn.

I remember the difficult times when I felt completely over-whelmed and unable to see past my present circumstances. I particularly recall the time one of Trent's community coaches left to take another job. Trent was left with no one. I was dealt several other negative circumstances at the same time: Trent lost his job at the YMCA, my divorce negotiations were failing, and Trent's brother Travis underwent chemotherapy for cancer. I think too much can happen to one person at once. My body began to shut down as all the crises hit me at once. I had no choice but to resign from my work.

I knew I had to take care of myself since I was responsible for Trent, Travis, and me. Each of us has his own way of taking care of himself in time of stress. I chose to rest in bed for seven days. I had no energy and I did not want to face any problems. If a problem came up during those seven days, I chose to not deal with it.

Fortunately, I chose to do one thing that helped immensely. While resting, I chose to read uplifting and inspiring books. One book from my educational courses in particular helped me shift my perceptions and actually pulled me through my grief. Seven

23

Habits of Highly Effective People written by Stephen Covey provided me the exact dose of therapy that I needed and was soothing to my soul.

I learned to evaluate principles by which I chose to live, and then to prioritize the principles in order to empower myself when considering choices. My paradigm shift confirmed for me that I do not have to be everything to everybody at all times. I learned that was a ridiculous way for me to think anyway. For the first time, I accepted the fact that I allowed my needs to come first. I accepted that it was OK to take a period of rest from my life due to the extreme demands placed on me.

Actually this time of reflection helped me recognize my feelings, my priorities, and offered me an opportunity to explore my next step toward meeting our goals. I realized as I grieved that I was experiencing certain stages of grief that I remembered studying in college. I recognized my feelings and labeled them. I began to understand the importance of my grief, which helped me eventually get past it. Of course, this sounds easy but it was difficult and it was not an overnight process.

What was I grieving? I grieved for the old secure family life I thought I once had. I grieved for the loss of my son. I grieved for the son who was supposed to have been born intelligent and fully competent. Surprisingly, I revisited grieving for Trent and the disability he had. I also grieved for my sons Todd and Travis who were continuously asked to help with Trent's care and who made compromises in the past. I grieved for all three of my sons and their loss for not having the kind of father I wished they had. I wanted my sons to have a father who supported, guided, provided discipline, and most importantly was available to share their struggles and joys. Yet, my sons were fortunate to have a father who provided financially for them. I learned later that I had to let go of my resentment toward their father so I could move forward with my life. Lastly, I grieved for the loss of my life. One of my deepest fears was that I would not be able to move forward in order to establish my independent life as other mothers who have nondisabled adult children.

It became clear to me that I was grieving with the same feelings I had years ago at the very time of Trent's diagnosis of autism. The emotions surfaced again during these transition years. During our family transitions and Trent's transition into adulthood, I relived and mourned old losses and memories from long ago.

Mourning The Old Life

From the kitchen I gazed into the family room and saw Trent sitting in his recliner, watching one TV program after another. The commercials were especially appealing to Trent as he exhibited excitement flapping his hands, vocalizing, and mimicking the exact words of each commercial. It was as if he watched the programs for the musical introduction and waited for the commercials.

I remember each day struggling to get Trent to leave the house for a walk or a bike ride. He adamantly refused. Before the unstructured days had arrived, the walking and the bike riding were the two activities I could always depended on Trent enjoying. I started to worry that he was regressing. Days later, I noticed Trent sitting for longer periods and it became even more difficult for me to get him to agree to leave the house. I wondered if he was feeling the unfamiliar uneasiness of his new life. I wondered if he missed not having a routine he could count on.

School provided the function of routine for him both of us. During school Trent found a routine that was acceptable and comfortable for him. I missed the structure that school provided Trent. I went through a period of reflecting on those days that were gone forever, a time when Trent seemed happy and content.

I remember the evening my mother and I went to a school program when Trent performed in the show choir before the entire school. That evening I felt nervous wondering if he would get upset, exhibit a public scene, and if he did what would I do? Trent sang every word to every song, the only singer rocking his body (an autistic characteristic) in perfect rhythm to the beat. In fact he had a peaceful, joyful expression and his face appeared more relaxed than ever before. After the performance, others approached me and commented that they enjoyed watching Trent perform. For the first time it was as if his autistic characteristic stood out in a most positive way.

I remember the night Trent went to his prom. It was important to me that Trent had ways to celebrate an ending to his school years. Going to the prom was one of them. How appropriate it was to celebrate the ending with other peers with food, music, dance, and dressing up. Erica, Todd's girlfriend had a real interest in Trent and offered to take Trent to the prom. Erica and I were excited about the evening and we made a complete night of it.

The prom night arrived. Trent was dressed in a fabulous black tuxedo with black shiny shoes. He cooperated in getting dressed up. Trent's dad drove us downtown to the hotel, but did not stay. Trent enjoyed the dinner and enjoyed the attention he received from some of his teachers. When other students came over to Trent and commented on how nice he looked, I felt such joy and peace was grateful that Trent played a role however so small in other's lives. This was the ultimate opportunity in belonging to a group. Trent truly had a place in this school and was living through an experience that was so typical for others. He truly belonged and others accepted him. Trent had his chance by going to the prom just as the others to say goodbye to his old life. I knew that saying goodbye would help bring his old life to a better conclusion as well as inspire him to be more open to a new life.

Those school days of precious memories were over. Life after graduation was very unsettling for both Trent and me. Any quality filled day required much effort and planning on my part.

Erica, Trent and Mom

I felt tired and overwhelmed as I arranged activities for Trent and searched for the person to serve as a community coach to him. When a community coach was found, I was involved daily in training the community coach.

My days were filled with working at the university, often meeting Trent and the community coach during my lunch break, rushing home each night motivating Trent to do something more than just sit and stare at the TV. I knew when Trent had increased unstructured time on his hands, behavior problems escalated. I thought about how I would cope with increased behavior problems, when I was already stretching myself managing Trent's immediate behaviors.

Trent desperately needed a routine. The community coach was with Trent for four hours a day and Trent worked four hours a week, but that was not enough to offer Trent a day of quality. I define quality as activities and persons who offer Trent a sense of "contributing" to his co-workers, family, friends, and an inner sense of contentment with his life. The real uncertainty for me was where was his life headed and I questioned how would his present life support the goal for independent living.

Would I have the energy and resources to arrange for Trent to access opportunities to learn independent living skills that would eventually help him find his place of belonging in the community? Was it realistic with all my limited energy, time, and resources to think Trent could ever reach the final goal of independent living?

I wondered with Trent's limited ability to communicate, what was going on in Trent's mind. I wondered if Trent missed the familiar contacts with those persons who were part of his everyday life during school. I wondered if he felt as unsafe about his life as I felt about both of our lives. I wondered if I would eventually lose the vision of independent living in future days to come. I wondered if Trent had fearful thoughts about what was next for him as he mourned the loss of his old life.

Again, it became clear to me that I was grieving the identical feelings I grieved years ago when Trent was very young. My emotions surfaced again during these transition years. Families living with children who are disabled go through various emotions as they experience the transition years. What were some of the emotions profoundly experienced?

Shock

The transition years can sneak up on you when you least expect it. A family soon realizes that the son or daughter will not have the security of school any longer. The impact may occur slowly, but when it does one still may not believe this is happening in the family.

The shock I experienced was a future warning that a family break up was headed our way. I had to accept the lack of support with our family break up would place all responsibility for Trent on me. Although I always have accepted that I would be the one developing Trent's day- by- day activities and choosing

the people who would coach Trent, I really did not fully understand the extent of the effort I would have to exert in order to
handle the inconsistent problems.

The shock set in for me after our family's break up and I did
not know what was next. I often thought, "What is my next
step?" I often couldn't believe all the things that were happening to me were really happening.

Many warning signs were sent my way so I would open my
eyes to see my reality. One particular sign occurred the last
school year before Trent graduated from high school. I experienced shock because I expected help from Trent's father resolv-
ing an issue that required me to keep my teaching job. Shock set
in when I discovered I did not have the support from him that I
thought I had.

Losing Trust

I remember the first day back teaching at the new school
year. The principal, announced a new policy at the faculty meeting. The first day for teachers every school year had always been
very chaotic and nervous for me. I not only had to prepare for
my students but I had to arrange for various details for Trent
such as preparing him emotionally to start a new routine, get
ready, meet the bus on time. So much had to be prepared for
Trent in order that he would accept the new school year.

I was sitting in the faculty meeting with all the other teachers, in the school library fumbling through papers, schedules,
and making notes to pass onto my students. The principal
announced that a new policy for teachers would be implement-
ed and no exceptions would be granted. All teachers must be in
the building no later than 7:00 a.m. working some form of hall
duty. Again he claimed that no one would be exempt from this
duty. My stomach ached. I did not know what to do. Trent's bus
never came before 7:00 a.m. and I would not have time to get to
school.

I called Mike during our first break and explained the new policy at school. I asked him to help me arrange care for Trent every morning until the school bus picked him up. Mike responded, "Jackie I can't. That's your problem. That is your job. You figure it out."

I left the school office to walk outside for an escape. I hoped no one would see my tears. I felt that I had too much to figure out alone and I recognized how low I felt when Mike spoke this way to me. When I needed him most of all he used those times put me down and place the blame on me.

Needless to say, I met privately with my principal and explained to him about Trent's needs and asked if I could make up my hall duty in some other way. He understood and made special accommodations for me. This particular situation and with many other similar ones, led me from trusting Mike and building a wall to avoid any more painful confrontations with him.

Denial at a Cost -
A Family Falling Apart

Let me make a case for denial just for the sake of argument. How denial lets you pretend that what is there is not really there. How it protects the status quo. How denial keeps everything in balance, however precarious, for a while anyway. How it allows life for the pretender to go on with just a slight adjustment, making room for that place where the dark hole of unacknowledged knowledge festers. How it allowed me to keep my jealousy from destroying me. How it allowed me to deal with an untenable situation without losing control. How I accommodated myself to it like one accepts a blind spot. How it kept me from collapsing. How Mike and I both accepted denial to protect our relationship and family. How we were both accomplices in denial: that which is not spoken does not exist.

I lived in a denial stage for years truly believing that Mike and I were both supportive of Trent's immediate and future needs for independent living goals. It took a long time for me to realize that Mike really did not have the same beliefs I had. I left the denial phase of my marriage on the morning of February 8, 1998,

Mike woke earlier than usual that morning and made coffee for us. I took a shower and got dressed for school. As I came downstairs to the kitchen, I felt a cold vibration in the air as Mike said, "Jackie, we need to talk. I spoke with Brian and I have agreed to accept the work in Columbus, South Carolina."

I knew he had already been offered the position in South Carolina, after his office here had closed. But I assumed up to now he would turn it down. I thought he would possibly accept a short- term position in South Carolina until the final position was determined. I asked, " How long will you be gone?" He answered with a low voice, "I'm moving there and we all will go." He lowered his head and puffed his cigarette. I stood there leaning against the refrigerator feeling sort of numb.

I thought this is the moment of truth. Within the past month we talked about his next position and visited other areas such as Chattanooga, Tennessee. But I was terrified about leaving Louisville. I could vision Trent and me being trapped in another town, trapped in our house, and never leaving except to go to the grocery store. I was afraid that I would not find anyone to stay with Trent in order to continue my degree or teaching. I spent a great amount of energy assertively seeking adult services for Trent, and I would now have to start all over again. And I knew Mike would not help. I knew so well I would be left alone to figure this out. That thought terrified me and I felt cold chills all over just contemplating moving with Mike.

I thought, "Did he not care? Did he not hear my desires to stay here where Trent would have services and I would have family support?" I thought he knew how important it was that Trent stayed in Louisville, because of his supports from the plans I put together for his life after high school. I had worked toward getting Trent connected and accepted into agencies for supported employment and for obtaining supported living grant. I knew I did not leave because of the doctoral course work I wanted to finish. Did Mike not see that accepting the job here in Louisville would keep our family together even though he would end up earning less money? Did he not see that moving to South Carolina would break up our family and leave Trent and me on our own? Did he not care?"

Trent was sitting in his big lounge chair waiting for the bus to arrive. I waited to respond to Mike after Trent left. I remember the distant, numb feeling that swept over my body. The kitchen was heavy with Mike's cigarette smoke. He had little respect for my nausea from the smoke. Travis and Todd had already left for school so Mike and I could talk freely after Trent left.

Trent headed out the door for the bus. I watched from the window as the bus pulled off. I walked into the kitchen feeling numb and angry, but still I did not let it out. I calmly said, "You know Trent and I cannot move 600 miles away to live a life of isolation for Trent and me. Are you going to leave us?" I noticed the choice of words I used- that is, Trent and me would be isolated, not Mike.

One thing I knew for sure was that the preparation and planning for Trent would always be mine to do. If supports were not there for Trent, then I would be the one isolated in the house. I knew Mike's work and Mike's life would never take a back seat to our needs.

Mike stared down at the newspaper as he sipped his coffee, and gave the same answer he had used over and over again for years, "It's business". His answer was like dropping a bomb on me. I had to walk. I ran out the front door and began to walk down the street. Walking helped me release and sort through my emotions. For a short time, I put my students who would be waiting for me out of my mind. I desperately needed to digest the news before I could go to school.

As I walked, I cried and I thought about all the times Mike left me before. We had never separated as husband and wife or as a family, but he had left me in other ways. When the kids were very young, ages seven, four, and one; and I made the suggestion that he and I go out that evening. Mike always responded to me as he was getting ready to go out with his friends, "You were the one that wanted to have these kids." We have them, stay home with them."

As I walked, I recalled back at the previous hurts in our marriage. Ten years after we were married, Mike awoke me at one a.m. to inform me that he had had an affair. That was all he said. He spoke with no remorse in his voice, as if he were reading a check-list or something. I wondered how many other times had he betrayed me.

I remember going over and over in my mind what my next step would be. I thought about leaving, but because of their ages I knew I could not provide the care for my three young boys Todd nine, Trent six, and Travis three alone. Although Mike was not much help, any kind of help he offered, was completely necessary for the daily care for the boys. Trent's autism, required much attention and care. I knew it would be nearly impossible to find childcare for him if I did get a job.

Although Mike worked long hours at the car lot and was rarely home with us, he still brought home security for our family. I believed that an uninvolved father was better than no father for my three sons. At that time I had no other help, no options I could consider, and no other place to go. So I chose to stay in the marriage at a tremendous cost.

Mike moved to South Carolina and worked there for eight months. He returned at Christmas time. However, he returned only to work at another job within his company. Although I believed we would be family again, it was only denial on my part.

The Lesson:
Letting Go of A Clouded Vision

I remember a time when I lived in denial about the support I thought Trent and I had. Seeing the truth was too difficult. Sometimes shock has to hit us hard in order for us to see the truth.

One late October evening Mike, Trent, and I were at Male High School watching Trent's brother, Travis, as he played football. I was so proud of Travis and his enthusiasm toward football. Watching him play was a thrilling experience for me. Other family members or friends often joined us. That evening, my mother was the only other family member with us.

A cool night breeze flowed past my face and through my hair. We were comfortable wearing light - weight jackets. The field lights shone brightly against the dark skies. We chose to find a seat off to the side and away from the cheerleaders and other action. We sat at the end of the lower half of the bleachers so if Trent had to leave he would not have to climb over people.

Travis and Trent

Mike never wanted to sit close to the cheerleaders where a lot of activities tended to occur. Although Trent may have enjoyed the cheers, he would sometimes surprise me when he became over stimulated and exhibited a noticeable characteristic of autism such as standing and flapping his hands. I would have chanced sitting near the cheerleaders, but I did not push my desires with Mike.

I appreciated the few times we all went out as a family. Mike and I had an unspoken agreement that when Trent was with us, we went out and did things on Mike's terms.

Mike always separated himself from us. Mike's detachment from me whenever we went out as a family was quite ordinary. Going out together as a family was rare. Our usual outings together involved mainly family gatherings. Mike's concerns were that Trent would embarrass him in some way. I always had Trent with me, which allowed Mike to keep his distance and his comfort. Little did I realize then that I played a role of helping Mike maintain his distance from us. Now as I reflect back I can see this distance was as being synonymous with rejection. That is, Mike rejected Trent and me. I often wondered if Trent felt Mike's rejection or did Trent just become accustomed to not having his dad's support and, therefore, he did not know what he was missing.

Louisville Male High School played against Ballard High School. Travis played on the defense for Male. That was a special game since both schools were equally favored to win. Mom and I chatted. This was the time I could tell her in more detail about my studies, and Trent's activities at school. Although Trent had his popcorn and coke and appeared satisfied and comfortable, I consciously held an inner peace within while preparing to react to any element of surprise by Trent and his behavior.

I gazed at the students walking with their friends past the bleachers. They were hanging out supporting their school, laughing and kidding around. I thought about Trent and wondered if he did not have autism, with whom would he be doing similar things. What would his style be? How would he dress? Would he be a trendy dresser and the jokester in the crowd? Would he dress preppy and have a quiet mannerism? Who would be his friends out in the crowd? How would he interact with his friends?

I stopped my thoughts and brought myself back to the reality of the moment because my thoughts made my heart drop as I felt sad for Trent and me. I suppose this is the guilt that seeps into my thoughts during various social experiences with Trent. It is odd, how guilt works. At times I think I have over come the guilt and fully accepted my circumstances with Trent and then it reappears again. I often felt sad for Trent. He did not have friends outside the classmates in his self - contained classroom. He did not have a group to which he could belong. He could not drive a car. He did not understand himself as an accepted friend or classmate. He even did not experience the support and pride that a father can give to his son.

I often worried about Trent's future. I accepted that Trent's reality at that time was one of exclusion. Within every fiber of my being, I have always held the dream that Trent would have independent living one day. And if I were ever to achieve independent living for Trent, I would have to arrange an additional support system for Trent. I knew I did not want to continue being everything to Trent. These thoughts would surprise and bother me. I often chose to push my future goals back on the shelf because I was not ready to deal with them.

Half-time had arrived. The score was 45 to 40 with Male High School ahead. Trent had been sitting on the bleachers now for over an hour and had become a little restless. He adamantly said, "Go bathroom." I asked Mike to take Trent to the bathroom. Mike answered, "Walk with us through the crowd, and you hold Trent's hand."

My mother, Trent, and I left the bleachers for the restrooms. Trent walked with me because Mike did not handle Trent's needs as well. Trent followed me cooperatively as we made our way through the crowd. I told Mike I would stand and wait for them by the fence. Minutes later, Trent hurriedly walked out of the bathroom toward me. Mike was right behind Trent. As they walked closer, I noticed Mike's jaw was squared and his lips

36

tightly pressed. Mike's eyes were blazed with anger. Mike yells, "What the hell is wrong with your son? Don't ever ask me to take him to the bathroom again." I asked, "What happened?" "Hell if I know, he started yelling and hitting the side of his legs." Mike answered. Then Mike yelled, "Get out of my face, get out of my life!" He walked away.

I immediately held Trent's hand and began to talk calmly to him. He was already calm because after he had an outburst he was relieved from his frustration. Chaotic environments and loud noise from the game stimulated Trent's senses and he became overloaded. It often became difficult for him to cope without the support from another person. Trent did not have the necessary support from Mike. Even when Trent was around supportive persons he could become upset from the setting and needed redirection.

That evening I remember thinking I would have to get out of my marriage. I realized that if I stayed with Mike he would never help me find a way to make Trent's life a life of independent living. I felt the emptiness in my chest and numbness all over my body with the new realization.

I always interceded by immediately reinforcing Trent's needs, thus preventing any further chaos or upsets between Mike and Trent. Mike rarely participated socially with Todd and Travis, Trent's two brothers. It was not surprising to me that he would not interact with Trent in public. Mike was afraid of the behavior that would stand out in front for all to see.

Mike chose merely to be present and not participate with us on certain occasions. I believe Trent felt Mike's rejection. I felt rejected and angry toward Mike whenever I saw Mike not supporting Trent. Only on a few occasions, when Trent was younger, I spoke firmly with Mike expressing my hurts and disappointments regarding his neglect toward each of us. However during this time of my life, I suppressed my thoughts rather than voiced them. I was living in the survival mode trying to deny how hurt and angry I really was toward Mike.

"How dare you think you have the mere right to just exist around us without your involvement. We are supposed to be appreciative of your presence? Your presence without acknowledgement of our needs is not OK. You are rude, disrespectful, and hurtful to all of us. You neglected us with your distance!" I thought. My body felt the results of my suppressed thoughts. During the time Trent was 18 to 22 years of age, I had these body symptoms: aching all over, frequent sinus infections, bursitis in my shoulder, viral meningitis, and weight gain of 50 pounds over my desired weight.

I eventually moved through the guilt and discovered some relief and hope for the new experiences we were about to encounter. I left the guilt behind and looked forward to a wholesome way of thinking.

What can a parent do when dealt with challenges that lead one to feel the guilt? One way I dealt with guilt included finding ways to compensate for our losses. Having guilt is all about having a feeling that you have lost someone or something. I started this process by asking what can be given back to balance what has been taken away in our family. I had overlooked this principle too long. My life was out of balance and I began to search for ways to stabilize myself.

As change came our way through the transition years, I learned that it affected each member of the family. When families living through the transition years choose to remain in modes of guilt, it drains energy from them. Living in guilt, led me to function well below my normal capacity. We continued to exist in the transition phase. It was a place where the future was yet to be established and completely unfamiliar to us. As our family entered the transition phase, anxiety arose and our motivation fell. I became disoriented and self - doubting as I tried to find solutions for new life after high school.

It took a long time for me to open my eyes and recognize

that Mike became resentful toward any change and protective of his familiar life. He refused to change and adapt to accommodate Trent's new life. I was blind to it all. I can now see the weaknesses in our family that were hidden for years. Continuing in this dysfunctional relationship would have kept Trent and me from leaving the transition phase. I did not manage this dilemma very well, but I eventually began to realize Mike was probably doing what he perceived as right behavior. I had to accept this to let go of the past and to move forward. Once I accepted this mindset, I began to notice changes. I felt empowered to make decisions about the changes I wanted for Trent and me.

Adult Day Care, Is It Appropriate or Just Functional?

This day in June started out bright with sunshine pouring through the kitchen sliding glass door. It had only been a week since Trent graduated from high school. I opened the door to let Bumper, our cocker spaniel outside. I had my books and notes that I had been studying for the past several weeks for my comprehensive tests for the doctoral program spread out over the kitchen table. I organized the books and notes to form neat stacks that would make it easier for me to later proceed.

This was a very focused summer for me. Each day I spent studying for my written exams. I only stopped to care for Trent. This was our first summer after Trent graduated from school. The school-structured day now was his past. My plans that summer involved Trent working at the grocery store and participating in the summer day program for adults with disabilities. On this particular day Trent started a summer adult day program, that I named Summer Camp.

I called for Trent from the bottom of the steps and reminded him for the third time to wake up and take a shower for Summer Camp. Trent yelled back, "Stay home." Giving him three more minutes, I waited to see if he would start on his own initiative. He refused to get up so I walked upstairs and stood there in front of his bed instructing him to put his feet on the floor. He immediately followed my instruction because he did not like me in his room.

After Trent ate his eggs and toast, he put on his shoes, and we left. I drove him across town to the summer program. It was convenient for me to drive Trent to the center because I had the summer off. I resigned from teaching and had accepted a new job with the Autism Community Training Project (ACT) at the University of Louisville. However, my new job did not begin until after I took my written exams.

Trent reluctantly got out of the car when we arrived. I always knew when he did not like going to a day program. After a brief walk inside the building, Trent slowly entered the huge room. I noticed the workers busily offering juice to the program participants and placing their book bags and lunch boxes away. As I looked around I noticed half of the participants in wheel chairs, and one young male was isolated and twirling around. I knew he had autistic characteristics. I was told there were three of the participants who had autism. Trent was greeted by one of the older male teenagers who happened to be the son of the director. I left Trent and encouraged him to have a good day.

When I arrived that afternoon, Trent noticed me and quickly grabbed his bag to leave. I asked the program assistant what activities did Trent do that day. It was the goal of the program to take the participants out in the community on an activity every-day. That is why I wanted Trent in the program. The woman answered, "Trent chose to stay at the center. He would not leave when we asked him to go with us." I replied, "You need to tell him it is time to go swimming, or it is time to go to the park." Please only offer him other choices regarding where to go before leaving. Trent will always choose staying back if that is one of the choices."

I wondered how much the program assistants understood

about autism. They should know that Trent would often make the choice to not participate. It was a great effort for me to travel downtown just to have Trent sit all day to work on puzzles. I strongly reminded Trent that he was suppose to go places and do things with the others in the program. I explained to him that was the reason that he was attending Summer Camp.

Several weeks passed and not much changed after that first day when Trent attended Summer Camp. I did not understand his lack of interest because while in high school he accepted the outings in the community with the other classmates. The program was not appropriate for Trent. I decided to withdraw Trent from the program after several weeks of trying to get Trent interested.

The Summer Camp served individuals by operating as a sheltered day program. Although the program offered community activities, the adults participated in the community activities within a large group, which drew attention to their disability. I believe that adult day programs have a functional use providing the participants certain activities to do and a place to go during the day. Unfortunately I believe these programs often send negative messages about people with disabilities. When a group of adults with disabilities participate in an outing or at a community event, it tells others that people with disabilities belong with their own kind, not with nondisabled persons.

I wondered why I even chose the program for Trent. It was clear to me that I was choosing to have that same comfort level that school offered. School served a function for me that filled Trent's day and I was subconsciously trying to hold on to that security. In fact, I believe I chose that security as a quick fix for meeting my needs to study for my tests and I was choosing that option at Trent's expense.

I also thought about how the Summer Camp program would not help us realize the goal for Trent to have independent living. Trent would not learn independent living skills if he were only exposed to working and participating with disabled individuals in sheltered environments. I withdrew Trent, without knowing the next step to maintain quality living for him. My focus shifted toward assuring that Trent work at the grocery store with supports so he would be able to maintain his job.

Saying Goodbye to Denial

It was a hot and humid July day. Dinner was almost ready. In between reviewing my notes for my tests to be taken in August and cleaning up the dishes, I prepared bacon and tomato sandwiches with coleslaw.

Mike walked into the kitchen and poured a tall glass of iced tea. I placed the dishes out on the counter for us to prepare our own plates. We had already stopped eating together as a family. Trent and I enjoyed eating our evening meal in the family room while watching TV. If Mike was home, he ate alone at the kitchen table.

I reminded Mike not to accept any job assignments in the second week of August when I would be taking my tests at University of Louisville. "I have a meeting in Chicago that has just come up." Mike answered. I could barely control my fury. "So you're refusing to follow through on your promise." I said.

"I cannot believe it. I arranged with you back in January to be here with Trent during my examinations. Again, you agreed to be here for Trent those three days. What do you think I have been doing all summer? Do you think this is a game I am playing? I have worked for three years to get to this point in the doctoral program. What do you suggest I do with Trent while I am taking my exams?" I announced. "Jackie, we all have work to do, ask your mom or someone. You will figure it out," Mike answered as he walked out the kitchen.

Another moment of truth had engulfed me. I had moved past the denial of expecting Mike to be there for us. I finally realized at that moment he would never be there for us. I recall thinking how I would manage staying with Mike through the end of my exams? I wanted out of the marriage, but I could not handle pursuing a divorce at that time. I knew had to stay focused on getting through just one more month. I chose not to allow Mike the satisfaction of discouraging my attention from my exams. No matter what he did or did not do, I decided to forge ahead. I felt unusually strong in spite of Mike.

One of the first things I did was to hire a community coach in August. He was about 27 years old. His job involved driving Trent to work and to various settings and events in the community in order to provide Trent an opportunity to learn various independent living skills. Some of these skills included: making purchases, shopping for clothes, personal items, and groceries. I also wanted the community coach to work with Trent on certain recreational skills such as exercising at the YMCA, going to the movie theater, eating in a variety of restaurants, and visiting the zoo.

I remember the day the manager at ValuMarket grocery store called me at the university to inform me that Trent had been sitting on the bench waiting for 20 minutes for his ride home. Trent became impatient and nervous about the wait and had an outburst, standing up to undo his pants. At that time in his life, when Trent experienced anxiety, he yanked on his pants, pulling them down. This was a brand new behavior he started to exhibit that summer. The manager pulled Trent aside and calmed him down.

I immediately left work to get Trent. I was so overwhelmed with all the responsibilities for meeting Trent's immediate needs and emergencies. Mike was never home during the week when we needed him. I worried how my supervisor felt about my leaving work in order to handle a small emergency.

As I arrived at the grocery store where Trent worked, the community coach had just walked in. He was 30 minutes late. He apologized to me and said it would not happen again. I spoke with him to explain that when Trent had even ten minutes of waiting his anxiety increased and behavior issues sometimes occurred.

The Lesson: Moving Forward with Fear

I lived in a state of shock after I became separated from Mike. I filed for divorce one week after Mike moved out of the house. It was a scary time in my life. I felt so wide-awake every moment. I wondered what had caused me to become so alert? Was I in such a numb state that I built walls around me so I sheltered myself from the depressing relationship I had with Mike? The pain was so unbearable that I had resorted to taking care of the daily business while blocking out my real feelings. Our relationship was dead and it had been for a long time.

Each day I lived on the edge. I began to pursue the adventurous choice of searching for a new way of living for Trent and me even if I had to turn my world upside down. As a result, I recognized I had made the choice to end my marriage with Mike even though I had no knowledge how I would manage providing care for Trent, financially supporting his needs, and finding another place to live that would be meet Trent's needs. Our house payment was excessive and although Mike was paying it, I knew I could not afford to continue living at the house. As I laid down each night I prayed for guidance because I was terrified about our future.

My mind raced with burdensome thoughts. Where would we live? How would Trent adapt to his new life? How would I adapt to my new life? How would I meet Trent's needs? What if I could not meet his needs because I had to work? When would I have freedom to have friends and a social life with Trent? Would any other man ever want to have me if I revealed that I had the responsibility of an autistic son? Although I would refuse to be friends with a man if he would not accept Trent, would I have to choose to be excluded from a normal life because of Trent?

At times I would let myself become overcome with grief. I felt sorry for myself thinking that I may never have the simple luxury to come and go as other single women who choose to leave their marriage. I wondered where are the open doors to my future? I felt as afraid for myself as I felt for Trent. And if something happened that I would not be capable of meeting Trent's needs would I give up on me? Would I have to basically give up my personal needs so that Trent could have his needs fulfilled? At times I sadly envisioned us living as a recluse from society.

The only answer for Trent to have his life and for me to have my life was for Trent to live without me in a supportive independent living arrangement. The only answer for Trent was that he needed to be free to explore who he was and his capability for growth. He could only achieve his potential in a life without total dependence on me. The only answer for me was to become free and to learn who I could become without being Trent's primary caretaker.

I wondered how I would ever make this happen financially? I barely had enough money coming in monthly to pay my basic expenses. The income I received from Trent's father combined with his supported living grant was not enough to hire a personal care attendant and other support persons for Trent.

I was eager to start my new life, but at the same time I was scared to death. When I felt depressed about my decision, I began to question my choice to divorce, asking, "Am I just being self-centered?" My thoughts fluctuated back and forth as I questioned my choice to end my marriage to Mike or to accept and stay in my bad marriage. But each time my heart told me I was heading in the right direction as I decided to move through the process toward ending my marriage. Even in the midst of being terrified, I felt a sense of comfort recognizing a quiet voice that affirmed for Trent and me that we would somehow be OK. I truly believed I was getting daily feedback from a higher power and that I was choosing the right path.

My days were packed with heavy responsibilities as I moved hurriedly and anxiously through my day. My work involved designing and leading an employment project for adults with autism and preparing and delivering trainings for educators.

Although it was stressful work it was rewarding. I enjoyed providing information and assistance to educators and families about autism and the transition years. But I was living a double life. On one hand I participated as an educational consultant assisting others and on the other hand I was living in the trenches with other mothers who were helping their children after graduation and were worried about their child.

I suppose my standards were high. I wanted Trent to have opportunities to experience community outings and community employment with nondisabled adults. I was against Trent participating in separate excluded programs such as sheltered workshops or day habilitative programs. I accepted the reality that some day I may be faced with certain circumstances whereby I may have no other choice but to place Trent in such programs. That was my real fear.

If I resorted to an adult day program or a sheltered workshop I knew Trent's opportunities to grow and live independently would become greatly limited. I saw these programs as dead ends for Trent in acquiring independent living. My goal was that as long as I could have my freedom to explore and grow in my life, I would strive to search for supports and receive services that would only increase Trent's opportunity for independent living.

I had high goals for Trent and myself. My goals seemed impossible to reach when my life became magnified with family crises. My personal crises became a demanding priority to face and Trent's daily needs came second.

I had to handle the difficulties of each day alone. While at work each day, I phoned Trent's community coach, to see how

Trent was doing. I remember worrying whenever the community coach had a difficult time getting Trent to leave the house for an outing or even just to put on his socks and shoes. I rushed home from work in the late afternoon. My second job began after picking Trent up at my mother's house. I had to prepare dinner after we arrived home, work late hours in the evening on my university assignments, and try to squeeze some time with Trent in the evenings for walks. The walks were a necessity to help relieve some of Trent's stored up energy from exerting little effort during the day. Many times I fell into bed completely exhausted. I did not realize at that time these would become routine days for over a year.

I was doing it all alone. I remember feeling pity for myself and even losing control with Trent at times. I felt really bad after I spoke harshly to him or neglected his needs so I could get rest. I cried in the shower and in my bed at night (to hide from my sons) asking how is this fair? I asked myself, "Am I crazy for trying to hold on to all these independent living principles that were embedded into me?" My research convinced me to believe so adamantly in independent living and in its principles.

I questioned, "Could I have been mistaken, about independent living?" What if the scholars who wrote about integrating the disabled into the community were observing and researching from a distance, and really had no clue about the real possibilities for its realization with individuals and their families. I often viewed scholars and other leaders as standing at a distance in their ivory towers proclaiming that persons with disabilities really can live in the community, participate in leisure activities, and even hold a job with natural supports from coworkers and their supervisors.

I thought at times I possibly was living out a make believe ideal world. Independent living was a great concept to write about but not really a workable plan. Everywhere in our community, I saw adult programs that separated individuals with disabilities from the nondisabled, or I heard from the families who still had their adult at home. Some of the separate programs included sheltered workshops, and day habilitation programs. I was confused and in need of help.

I was ready to start my new life, but still lived within the transitional phase. How could my family manage temporarily until we found the new way of life? I discovered the solution was to create a temporary system of family functioning.

Creating A Safe Temporary Place within The Transition Phase

Consider this question. What new roles and new relationships do families need to develop in order to move through the transition phase into the new life? I learned to accept help when help was offered.

Soon after I became separated from Mike, I had to decide where to live. When it came time to consider where Trent, Travis, and I would live, I considered my options. I considered an apartment and wondered how Trent would adapt? Trent enjoyed playing his music loudly. He was use to a large physical space to move about in the house and outside in our yard. Trent was a floor pacer. He paced when he listened to music. He paced when he watched TV. I worried if neighbors in an apartment complex would accept Trent. He would become more visible and at times Trent would show his autistic behavior that might not be acceptable. What if Trent tore his shirt or became obsessed outside for long periods of time with a leaf or a stick on the ground. I was worried about how others would react? Would we be talked about? Would other families be fearful of Trent or even ridicule him?

One evening my mother phoned to invite Trent and me to dinner. Mom was always there for me when I needed her. She would welcome Trent over at her house when I had no one else to care for Trent or when I had to work or attend a class at the university. Mom was a small petite lady with dark short hair and wide brown eyes. She spoke with an upbeat tone in her voice and had a total recognition of Trent and his needs. She often spoke to Trent as if he was a small child and that bothered me especially when we were out in a restaurant. I wanted others to see Trent as an adult. When she spoke to him as if he were a child, it conflicted with my intent to treat him as an adult. Trent loved his grandma and peered over her like a gentle giant. He was also gentle with her whenever he reached out to hug her. Although she spoke to him as a child, Trent gave her lots of eye contact and smiles.

Grandmother Griffin

Shoneys restaurant was one of Trent favorite restaurants. He loved eating hamburgers and french-fries. After we had eaten most of our food, I sensed something was on my mom's mind. Mother hardly ate her dinner and merely picked at her salad. She quickly glanced at me and looked down again at her food while nervously moving her hands and fumbling with her fork. Mother always made me nervous when she acted like this because I knew she had something important on her mind. Mother did not make a big deal out of things like the rest of us. She never showed us that she worried. She always saw the positive outlook of every situation that she and her children faced. Likewise, mother always chose the appropriate time to tell us anything new. She would even withhold news whether is was good or bad if it was not the appropriate time to tell. I calmly asked Mother what was on her mind.

Mother looked up from her salad and smiled. She spoke yesterday with Sandy, the daughter of Mrs. Nash, the elderly 92 year - old lady who lived in the house next door to my mother. Sandy told mother that she was placing her mother in a nursing home and she would put the house up for sale soon. Mother told Sandy to let her know before she placed the house for sale because she knew that I might want the house for Trent, Travis and me. Mother asked me what I thought about living in the house next door to my brother and her.

I felt my stomach drop as my heart began to beat hard when I heard the news. I glanced over as Trent dipped his french-fries so carefully in the ketchup and his eyes expressing delight with each bite. I excitingly expressed to mother that I would love to live in that house.

Ms. Nash's house would be a wonderful place to live. It was a basic wood frame house in the earlier days, but Mr. Nash made many home improvements throughout the years. He built a large second floor dormitory with pine wood floors, a huge family room with built in bookcases, a fireplace, and extended the kitchen.

I realized that I could not afford the house. First, I did not have the money for a down payment. Second, I was not yet divorced and was not sure if a bank would give me a loan while I was still married to Mike. I told mother disappointingly that I would love to live next door to Craig and her. Mother said that she had thought about it and suggested that my brother Craig might want to buy the house and rent it to me. Mom suggested that I stop in to ask Craig. I was reluctant to ask him for such a large favor.

We are all unique in our own individual way, but Craig is exceptionally unique. Craig never married and after getting out of the army when he was 23, he found a job at the post office. He lived with my mother, and looked after her. Craig is a very

Uncle Craig

quiet man, and rarely initiates a conversation, but when he speaks he has something important to say. Craig has few friends, but his close friends have been so for over 25 years. In his pastimes, he prefers to spend time alone and enjoys attending various spectator sport events.

Trent actually saw their home as his second home. That is the one place that has never changed as my mother has lived there for over thirty years. It has always been known as Grandma's house from the time of Trent's early child hood.

I decided to ask my brother for help. One week later, I arranged to go into work one hour late. Craig worked the evening shift at the post office and was usually home during the work week mornings. When I walked in the house my brother was on the phone with his legs crossed in his favorite chair watching the morning news on television. I waited nervously as he finished his call to a friend.

Craig knew I was pursuing a divorce from Mike. I told Craig that I needed help. I could not afford the house payments and had to move out of our house. I needed a place for us to live. I mentioned to Craig how Mother learned that Sandy was selling Ms. Nash's house. I asked Craig if he would consider purchasing the house and renting it to me. I continued talking nervously not giving him a chance to answer.

My brother had been in the army years ago and had never purchased real estate in order to use the Veterans loan. I believed he had saved most of his income because he has always lived modestly. In fact, the only large item he ever purchased was a car.

I explained to my brother how I investigated the Veterans Home Loan with a friend of mine in real estate. The Veterans Home Loan would require no down payment. I assured him that no extra money would come from him by purchasing the house. I would pay the monthly rent required to cover his house payment. I would pay for the home inspection and any small repairs needed to pass the loan approval. My brother looked down at his newspaper without giving me any eye contact. He merely nodded his head up and down to indicate, yes. That was it. I asked him, excitingly, "Are you saying you will?" He answered, "Yes."

I tearfully thanked him and told him I would never forget how he helped me during one of the most critical times of my life. Indeed, his assistance was one of the most generous and kindest ever bestowed on me. I was elated and relieved. I cannot think of another time I felt so safe and protected. I could not have moved to a better place in town that involved help and support for Trent. Although my standard of living significantly dropped I was extremely happy. I moved from a two-story brick home to a small wood-frame house in a working class neighborhood where I lived as a child. I ironically felt I was moving forward in my life and at the same time going back to my roots. It was comforting.

I was grateful to him as he offered us an open door when we desperately needed one. Surprisingly, my new circumstances offered me an opportunity to empower myself. The move proved to be the new step that was essential for getting Trent and myself through the transition stage.

Living next door to my brother became the temporary system and the catalyst for reaching our goal of independent living for Trent. In retrospect as I now see the bigger picture, I recognize this option was a major short-term choice that led to our long-term plan for Trent to eventually meet the goal of independent living. Several years later the house next door to my brother became Trent's independent home with another young man who supported Trent as a living assistant.

Denial and Protection

Some families may have a difficult time accepting the end of their child's high school years. They may not have planned effectively for services, such as, choosing adult care, transportation to the job site, or worse the long empty days ahead for their son or daughter. On the other hand, there are families who may have a difficult time actually visualizing their son/daughter's potential to work and live in the community. Some families may refuse or cannot see how their son or daughter could be trained to ride the public transportation independently, or hold a job with natural supports.

Why do we parents sometimes refuse to see their children's potential? We are so used to protecting and advocating for our children. We hold an underlying fear that our children could get hurt or they might even not need us in the same way that we were once needed before as parents. Whatever the case, it is difficult for families to move forward and to make plans when they remain in the stage of denial. Until I could either see our future and appropriately plan or determine Trent's potential for working and living in the community independently, my denial stage continued to prevent us from adapting.

I remained in denial about preparing for my son's life after my death. Some families (including mine) deny that there will eventually come a day when one or both parents are not capable of caring for their disabled adult child. Plans for guardianship and writing a will and a trust are highly significant actions that a family must take. Although I knew I should be doing these things, it was not until I took a trip to Panama with a close friend and Trent was 23 years old, that I found the courage to make arrangements for Trent after I am deceased. It finally hit me after my divorce that I was Trent's only constant companion and the sole person responsible for any services or resources he received. Without thorough planning, I would have no say about how Trent would live after my death. My point is, I lived in the denial stage and I fully understand why families place these responsibilities on the back burner.

The transition years require families to often seek services in an assertive way. I know of some families who assumed that there were available services for their adult child just by placing a phone call. These families sadly heard a cold wake up call when they encountered long waiting lists or additional lengthy steps to acquire services. Families need to be aware of this process and stay informed to obtain adult services.

Trent Resists The Winds of Change

The first month Trent began living independently was emotionally draining for him as well as for me. He began exhibiting behaviors that communicated to me that he was slipping into a depression. I checked in on him daily via phone and drop in visits. It was all so new to me. On the one hand I sensed that I was the director of the "Trent Altman independent living agency" responsible for every need for Jason and Trent. On the other hand, I was caught up in the emotional turmoil of letting go of my special son.

Never before in our lives had Trent and I lived apart. I was overwhelmed with organizing and budgeting the dollars needed for Trent's daily living arrangement. My responsibility involved running out to stores purchasing necessary and unexpected household items. My dollars were limited. I had to stretch my financial resources to keep up two households and pay Jason's salary.

I frequently asked myself, "Why am I here?", as I entered my unfamiliar apartment each night and tried to settle in. I had never lived alone for 46 years of my life. My emotions were mixed with every hour that I spent alone in my apartment. On one hand, I was thrilled to have the independence to come and go as I wished. For the first time in my life I experienced privacy and relief from the care of Trent. Yet on the other hand, I was stressed from all the mixed emotions and with the anxiety of letting go of Trent. It was difficult for me to get use to idea of not being Trent's primary caretaker, the one person whom he knew understood his wants, needs and desires. Now Trent was left to respond on his own, relying on Jason for assistance.

One week after Trent began his independent living, he developed an ingrown toenail and needed medical care. The podiatrist Trent had visited frequently was not in when I called for an appointment. Trent was scheduled to see a different doctor. I was concerned about having an unfamiliar doctor treat him because changes were occurring all around Trent. Having a different doctor treat him was another added change.

Trent's visit to the doctor proved to be a devastating experience and one I will never forget. My intuition was on target. The doctor suggested that Trent needed surgery to remove the toenail. Trent cooperated fully with the nurses and the doctor by sitting still, accepting the shot for the numbing of the toe, and wrapping the toe in a bandage. It seemed that the doctor's visit was going to be successful. However, after the bandage work was completed, Trent quickly jumped out of the chair and charged across the room to the biohazard box and shouted, "blue." Jason immediately, grabbed Trent, to prevent him from getting into the box.

Jason informed Trent about the dangers of the box and then switched the topic to leaving the office and heading for the car. Trent refused to leave the room or even give Jason eye contact. Jason and I tried to analyze what Trent wanted. I thought about all the times Trent found pleasure in tearing empty food cartons into tiny pieces before letting them drop into the trash. I was sure that Trent had become fixated on a particular item.

The nurse began to tell Trent about the dangers of the items in the box when I asked her what was blue in the box. She replied that the container holding the needle was blue. She left the room and brought Trent another blue container hoping that would satisfy him. Unfortunately, it did not work. I intervened and asked if she could please remove the box from the room. After she left with the box, Trent loudly repeated, "blue!" and tried to leave the room when Jason stepped in between the door and Trent.

Each time we tried to get Trent to walk down the hall to leave, he tried to turn the opposite direction toward the other offices. We knew he wanted to search the other rooms for the biohazard box. Trent was so fixated on his desire to find the biohazard box, he refused to listen to our requests. After about one hour and a half of confinement to the room, the doctor entered and suggested that Trent be removed physically. Jason did not have the ability to physically remove Trent because Trent was a large man 5' 10" weighing about 230 pounds. Jason suggested that I call someone to help. The doctor informed us that if we could not get help, they would have to call EMS and that would involve taking Trent to a treatment center whereby he would be held and evaluated for 72 hours.

Immediately, tears welled up in my eyes. I thought about how doctors still did not understand autism. Didn't the doctor know that Trent did not have a mental illness, rather he had autism which was a developmental disability?

I turned to Jason and told him I would try to get someone here to help. My sons were not reachable. Trent's father was working out of town. I just started dating a nice man, but I did not feel comfortable yet calling him for emergency assistance.

At last I reached my brother-in-law Pat, who arrived twenty minutes after I called. Pat tried to tease Trent and trick him into leaving. Trent was not responsive to Pat. At that time, Pat grabbed one of Trent's arms and Jason the other, leaving quickly, they drug Trent out the door through the waiting room. I remember thinking how embarrassed I was for Trent. Although people in the waiting room did not know Trent, this scene was so negative and I thought about how this experience would portray persons with disabilities in a negative way.

As soon as Trent was escorted to the car, he relaxed, was calm, and showed no effects of the experience. It was as if in the doctor's office he was trapped, physically locked into retrieving the biohazard box. He could not literally unlock himself. Never had Trent exhibited such an extreme behavior before. In fact, he had always been able to follow through with any request. Unfortunately, this was the worst situation we have ever encountered. Trent began exhibiting obsessive behaviors for the next few months whenever he left a public place.

I realized the doctor did not understand autism. How traumatic it would have been for Trent if EMS had taken him to a facility for 72 hours of observation. Although I was Trent's legal guardian, I was told I would not be able to do anything about it. For the following months, Jason and I worked together planning the interventions when we were out shopping. Often Jason and I had to escort Trent out of a public place. Trent's obsessions began to decrease as Jason became more persistent with the behavior management. Trent improved in his adaptation to his new life.

I believe that with all the changes and with the falling apart of our family, it was too much for Trent to handle at one time. Experiencing all the changes, Trent regressed and he needed help to cope. Due to Trent's limited ability to fully communicate he was not capable of expressing his feelings. I visited him daily and I spent most of my weekends with him. Eventually, Trent began to understand and see that I had not abandoned him.

Although it was difficult at that time to see Trent's growth, I later looked back and saw that Trent made substantial growth just facing the changes and crises for the past year. Any of us would have experienced setbacks faced with similar changes that Trent endured, however, our effects of the setbacks would have been visible in different ways. Trent's symptoms of depression were related to the crises, not an effect of his autism. Rather I understood that his autism merely became larger in a time of change and crises.

Trent Surrenders to His Grief

For the first time since Trent had begun to live independently, I saw Trent grieve the loss of our lives living with each other in our home. On Thanksgiving 2000, Trent began to see a ray of light and the acceptance of his new life. This is our story.

Thanksgiving was a very happy holiday because so many positive changes were happening in my life. I had just gotten married two weeks earlier, and Ralph, my new husband, and I wanted to share the holidays by having my family over for dinner. We arranged to have Trent come early that morning about 9:00 a.m. so he could share in the food preparation activities. Trent loved to help us prepare food, by chopping vegetables, pouring, mixing, stirring, and cooking. There was plenty to do. Along with the cooking we played Trent's favorite CD's. As we cooked, we sang, and danced to some of Trent's favorite music.

The rest of the family arrived about 3:30 that afternoon. I was somewhat nervous about our day hoping it would go well since this was the first time Ralph and I had my family in our home. My other sons, Todd and Travis and their girlfriends came for dinner. They were friendly and courteous, although they were a little unfamiliar with Ralph. The day went especially well as everyone celebrated in cooking, talking, laughing, and eating. Later that evening everyone left full from eating and content.

After I cleaned up the dishes, I drove Trent back to my mother's house where he spent the night. I sensed that Trent was very uneasy. After we arrived to my mother's house, I stayed and chatted with my mother and brother about a half an hour.

When it was time for me to leave, Trent did not want me to go. He pulled me into my brother's bedroom. Trent was free to go into his room anytime because there was a TV for him to watch whenever he chose to watch a different station. He sat on the bed and gazed down and tears welled up in his eyes.

Trent rarely cried. I held him without saying a word through my own tears. A few minutes later, I began to talk to him about the day and the joy we shared. I thanked Trent for spending time with me and helping me all day with the cooking. I began to tell him that I have a new husband and reminded him that my new husband will not take away our relationship. I reminded him that I would always be his mother and I would always be there for him. I gave him examples of how we will continue to spend our time together, reinforcing how our old life would merge with our new life.

I talked with Trent's about his new life in his own home with Jason. I explained how he had a right to have his own life just as his brothers do. I affirmed that I was the one responsible for making all of his new independent living happen. I assured Trent that I was the one who found Jason and I planned and made independent living happen. Most importantly, I explained that I planned his new life to live independently because I loved him so much.

Trent held me tight and I did not let go until he was ready to let go. Looking back on that Thanksgiving night, I realized that Trent moved closer toward accepting his new life. He expressed his feelings of sadness, which would eventually allow him to heal from the despair and move into his future. I could not protect him or prevent any grief or sadness he encountered. I recognized that Trent had to experience the sadness just as I experienced the sadness from letting him go.

Trent's Work Experiences

Trent has had several opportunities on various jobs with nonhandicapped co-workers. Some of his job sites were good job matches for Trent, yet did not work well because they did not provide the necessary supports and understanding he needed from his co-workers and supervisor.

Two things were needed to determine if a job would work well for Trent: 1) a job that must be a good match to Trent's interests, and skills, and 2) a job wherein the job setting, tasks, and co-workers met his strengths as a worker and understood ways to help him adapt and learn his job. When developing a job, a job coach does not just search for a business with vacancies. But the job coach seeks a job that addresses the supports Trent requires from having autism as well as his personal unique needs. These concerns are critical for Trent's success in maintaining the job. Several of the methods used to determine Trent's skills, interests and needs were:

- review of his high school work experiences,
- interviews with family members/teachers,
- observations of Trent working at the job site,
- and trial and error assessments.

The areas that were assessed included his basic work skills, communication skills, social skills, his vocational preferences, his learning style, and most importantly, his behavior challenges. Special attention needed to focused on:

- nature of job tasks
- job complexity
- number of job tasks
- need for flexibility
- environmental factors

From the time Trent graduated from high school he had four jobs: Value Market grocery store, the YMCA, Papa Johns Pizza, and K Mart Department Store. There were similarities and differences with each job.

Value Market Grocery Store

Trent worked well in the produce and placed fruits out for display. In the back of the store Trent bagged candy and sorted through fruit determining rotten from the ripe in order to place on display. He liked his job, but he had to leave the job because we moved across town and transportation was not convenient to get Trent to work.

YMCA

Trent gathered the dirty towels in the men's locker room and moved the large cart of towels to the laundry room, where he washed, dried, folded, and put the towels away. Trent worked very well to everyone's surprise. After about one month, Trent became used to the routine and the job tasks. One day ten minutes before Trent's shift ended, a co-worker took Trent to the basement to retrieve an item. Trent became very upset and agitated. He was taken off his routine. Trent thought he only had ten minutes left to work and starting a new and unfamiliar task threw him off. Trent eventually had to leave this job because of the difficulty with the disrupted routine.

Papa Johns

Trent folded pizza boxes at Papa Johns. Although he seemed to enjoy the work, Trent was beginning to develop extreme obsessive behaviors whereby he wanted to adjust boxes and cleaning containers in perfect order. At the same time, Trent was beginning to show obsessive behaviors whenever he was out with me shopping. The obsessive behaviors caused Trent to lose his job.

Trent's person - centered planning team met several times to brainstorm and determine interventions, supports, and the appropriate work environment Trent needed for his next job. At this particular time, we determined that finding him a job would be postponed until later. I had been making arrangements for

Trent to live independently with support from Jason his living assistant. For Trent to adapt to the big changes of living without his family, work at that time was not the highest priority. Trent had to adapt to living with Jason.

Kmart

Several months after Trent had been living independently, he started a job a K mart. Trent needed support to learn his job. Jason had become familiar with Trent's strengths and needs and was hired along with Trent. Both Trent and Jason worked in the lay away department. They moved, arranged, and retrieved lay away items at Christmas time. The job tasks worked well. It was an ideal situation for Trent.

After Christmas, Trent's supervisor wanted both of them to work in processing shoes. The job was to pull out paper, arrange the shoes a particular way in the box. Trent did not like the task. After he worked at the job for a few days, he became very upset and Jason had to take Trent home.

The supervisor and co-workers at K mart appeared to understand so I suggested that Trent's job coach explore the option of a different job for Trent. The supervisors at K mart were extremely understanding and supportive. They offered Trent a job in tagging clothing. I will always remember that day and the blessing Trent and I received.

Trent Is Accepted

I will always remember that day at Kmart as I waited anxiously for Jason and Trent to arrive. We planned to meet with the team to determine another job for Trent. I had reflected back on Trent's last day at the job. The job task assigned to him was inappropriate because he was unable to work through the task of shoe processing. The task involved multiple steps that were confusing. Trent became very upset with the task. Jason reported to the supervisor over a month ago that the job was not right for Trent.

Barry Whaley, Director of Community Employment

Barry, the director of Community Employment, Troy, the job coach, Jason, Trent and I had arranged to meet with Trent's supervisor, and the district manager. Our plan was to explain how a nontraditional job would be appropriate for Trent. The

Job Coach, Troy Klabor

team explained the strategies for carving an ideal job for Trent. We determined Trent would require these supports:

• flexible working hours,
• one particular repetitive task that was not time dependent for its completion
• Jason hired along with him for support.

As I waited for Jason and Trent I prayed for divine intervention to take place in this meeting, "I will accept whatever the outcome becomes. I trust a solution is found. If it is meant for Trent to have the job - then I accept. If not, then I will look for the next step."

As the meeting began I sensed Trent was a little uneasy, but he appeared cooperative. Trent's supervisor welcomed Trent back. Trent responded with a smile as he greeted her quietly. Sharon asked us to enter the meeting room and have a seat around the table. The conference room appeared to be too small to hold a meeting, but there was a table and enough chairs for everyone. When Barry and Troy arrived I introduced them to everyone. Shortly thereafter, the district manager arrived. Troy, Trent's job coach opened the meeting by asking me to tell the team our purpose for meeting.

I summarized the issues of Trent's last day at work that led to Trent leaving early. Jason then explained in further detail Trent's upsetting experience with the shoe processing job task. I then explained that Trent possibly failed at the new task because he needed an introduction to the task prior to starting the new task. Trent sometimes needed several short periods of working on the task in order to adapt to the task and the new part of the building. I explained that Trent was not prepared for his last job. I also explained that Trent needed his employer to understand his ability to hold a job was dependent on flexible work hours, and a job task tailored for his unique needs for repetition. He required work that was not based totally on his productivity. Rather, he needed a task he could do repetitively and where time dependency was not an issue.

Everyone sat still. Not a word was spoken from anyone for several seconds. Those seconds seemed like minutes. I felt a gentle calm flow like a continuous warm stream through me. My heart beat softly. I thought of the prayer I said earlier and I was grateful.

Barry asked the district manager if there was a job task at Kmart that was repetitive and not time sensitive. We were seeking a task that did not have to be completed within a time frame but a task that needed to be completed. Trent's supervisor's eyes suggested that she was not aware of any job task like that.

She asked the district manager if he had any suggestions. Barry broke the ice by interjecting, "No pressure on you." We all laughed. Trent sat still and appeared to be carefully listening to the dialogue, by offering quick gazes to Barry and Troy then gazed back down to his hands again. The district manager answered, "We could try Trent in soft clothes processing. He could tear the plastic from the clothes and tag clothes." Barry asked if we could see the area where Trent would work and the kind of work he would do.

After we examined the work setting, we met back into the meeting room to discuss the hours Trent would work. I felt a sense of peace and thanked God in a silent prayer. I thanked every participant at the table for meeting. Barry turned to Trent and asked if he wanted to come back to work at K mart. Trent responded, with a quiet raised voice, "Yes", then he reached over and gently placed his head on my shoulder and reached out for my hand.

Trent and I were granted a blessing and I was thankful.

Part Three

DESIGNING AN INDEPENDENT LIVING ARRANGEMENT

Security

What does security mean to you? Take a look at this list. Consider what brings security to you. Which ones do you utilize to ensure that you have security in your life and your young adult's life?

- Predictability in activities your young adult participates
- Persons who associate and instruct your young adult,
- Services and quality in your young adult's life.
- Being loved
- Good health
- Independence (yours and your young adult)
- Autonomy
- Belonging
- Free choice
- Love
- Financial security that will support your young adult's quality of life now and after you die

In order to focus and achieve these securities, one must recognize the myths that are negative messages we often hold on to and believe. I want to share with you some myths I once believed to be true and have heard other parents say about independent living. These myths are synonymous with fear. Essentially I recognized that we parents have certain fears about letting go of their young adult. After experiencing 20 plus years of providing care, guidance, and protection for Trent, I know how difficult it was to surrender to an unknown new way of life. If I had listened and believed some or any of these myths, independent living would not have become our reality today. Lets look at a few:

- Independent Living cannot work without an agency
- Independent living won't work for my daughter
- It will mean changing everything
- The state (not parents) should provide an agency to arrange independent living
- Let's just wait until our son is ready
- It is too expensive and where are we going to get the money
- It's too risky, and I do not trust people
- I'll think about it later or a few years from now.
- Somebody would have started it before in our community if it were any good
- We don't have the time to design it
- Not now
- What's the rush?
- Let's not move too fast
- My son is too disabled, he has autism and cannot communicate his own needs
- It's just too soon to start independent living

A False Sense of Security

Some families may say they want independent living for their adult, but actually choose to keep their son or daughter at home because they are unsatisfied with adult services and long waiting lists. Families may choose the safer route even if it is painful rather than venturing into the unknown. The family may become so overwhelmed by the prospect of what might happen if they were to choose independent living that they cannot even begin. Their primary motivation is the desire to avoid pain or fear and to maintain their comfort and safety as they know it.

Personally, I felt all the fears and pain of surrendering Trent to independent living. However, I was motivated by risk to let Trent go, and to provide freedom and solitude for both of us. There are many families for whom safety means keeping their child from working in order to have the maximum Social Security Income (SSI) in order to pay basic expenses.

How we define safety depends on our personal values as well as where we are in our lives. Our pattern for managing this safety through our many life changes is uniquely our own. For example, I am excited by change as long as it is good change. How does your family intend to manage safely through your life changes? How do you intend to manage safety for your young adult through his life changes?

Here are some exercises to try to determine how you manage safety.

A. Visualize yourself at the end of your journey of letting go of your young adult to independent living. A few years ago, I visualized letting go of Trent and all I could see was a picture of myself at the edge of a cliff. The feeling I had was one of terror and that if I took one more step I would fall into the deep hole below.

B. Now add something to the picture you are visualizing that would make you feel safe enough to take another step. I visualized a mountain of pillows from the bottom of the deep hole to the top of the cliff so that if I fell I would be protected by their softness. I realized the pillows represented steps I needed to take to feel safe enough to begin. For me the steps meant finding information about 1) supported employment programs, 2) supported living grants, and, 3) federal community programs and services ranging from subsidized housing, to Medicaid. Equally important, it meant that I find professional people, friends, neighbors, etc., who would help Trent and me find independent living options.

C. What are your family's limitations to achieving independent living for your young adult? Do they involve money? Or knowledge? If you are knowledgeable about services and your son's needs to live in the community but lack the funding to hire qualified persons available to work with your son, you have fewer limitations than someone who doesn't know about services or programs.

D. What stops you from exploring independent living?

You may believe one of the following statements:

1. If I surrender my son to independent living and he becomes sad about not living with us anymore, I will feel guilty and sad. I will feel I have abandoned him.

2. If I let go of my daughter to independent living, my family may not support me, I may lose my family, and the status quo of our family structure.

Now reflect on several different kinds of statements that may actually do your young adult an extreme disservice. These may be some of the statements you are making.

A family comment:

My choice is to have my son live at home. When I get ill or die, I suppose an agency will take him then.

My answer:

If you choose to live with this belief you are throwing caution to the wind. There are very few agencies that offer community living and the waiting lists are so long. It may take years before an agency gets to your young adult's name. If you get ill or die and no one is there in the family to care for your son in the home, it is likely your young adult may become a ward of the state and be placed by the state in an institution or other facility.

A family comment:

My choice is to have my son live at home and allow one of his sisters or brothers to take care of him if ever I get sick or die.

My answer:

Depending solely on the siblings who will care for the young adult after your death is not a guarantee either. Although you may have children that love and want to care for their disabled brother, they may have to focus on their own immediate family needs for several reasons:

• An already established work/life in another city/state.
• Family issues and children issues that are foremost.
• Lack of time and resources to attend or care for the sibling with a disability.
• Possible health issues and other family crises and burdens.

Sometimes families have siblings that may have the time and resources to care of the disabled family member. However, many siblings find work in other states and have their own family issues to handle.

I have chosen NOT to shift my responsibility of Trent's future care, planning, and preparation to my other two sons upon my death. I saw planning and preparation for Trent's life as my responsibility NOW. I choose not to place that enormous responsibility of care and planning on Todd and Travis. I have however, planned in my will, a request that Todd and Travis act as guardians for the decision making in all the areas of Trent's life and the facilitation of Trent's independent living arrangement.

It was my intention to prevent any added responsibilities on Todd and Travis regarding the care of Trent. By immediately placing Trent initially in independent living while I was healthy and capable of making decisions and arrangements, will help cushion those times for all three of my sons when crises come our way. My sons would be relieved from figuring out where Trent would reside, who would care for his needs, and the necessary supports needed to have in place.

Another reason to place the young adult in community living early is because it is easier for the individual to adapt to independent living. Research from the *Autistic Spectrum by Lorna Wing* indicates that the earlier the adult individual lives in the community, the better the person with a disability is capable of adapting to the new life. I realize I cannot consider every possible situation to plan for Trent's independent living after I am gone, but I have peace knowing that Trent has adapted to living without total dependence on his family and I have not left Todd and Travis with the complete responsibility.

A family comment:

It is my choice is to keep my son at home after high school. If I get sick or die, then someone will have to get an agency to take him and teach him community living skills and job skills.

My answer:

There are no instant guarantees that your adult would instantly have access into an independent living arrangement. It will depend on when your family crises occurs and how progressive the state has moved forward in this area. However, blindly counting on such support is not very smart or even a very caring thing to do when it comes to your young adult's future. State community living lists are long and the likelihood your young adult getting into an agency may still be rare even in later years.

Let's consider again about how well your young adult may adapt to independent living upon your family crises. Just suppose for a moment that an agency is ready and willing to accept your son into community living upon your death. Your son may be 35, 47, or 60 years old at your death. What do you think his adaptive level will be at any of these ages to the community to learn new skills? How adaptive do you think your family member is for handling the death of a parent when all he knew for years was that parent caring for him? Many families sadly do not choose to provide preparations for their young adult. When crises arise, the family may become paralyzed and may not know where to turn or what to do.

Try Believing in This

I discovered that I had to begin thinking of possible ways that I could surrender Trent to independent living several years before I was willing to accept the idea. I remember repeating convincing thoughts to myself.

> "Life is ever changing for my family and each member of my family and that includes my disabled son. Everything that happens to me is happening for a reason. I am doing exactly what I'm supposed to be doing right now. I'm just too close to it to understand the benefits of our struggles."

Take one step at a time. With every step I took, I believed that I increased my own security.

Start Today

Wherever you are begin your young adult's future and your future now. Planning and preparation can never start too early. Planning should and can begin today. Your planning may involve taking just one small step. That step may include allowing your young adult to attend a baseball game with a neighbor, networking to find and hire a community coach to introduce leisure activities on weekends to your daughter. Or you may start to plan by taking any of these action steps:

- obtain guardianship of your young adult.
- complete an application for the state's Medicaid Supports for Community Living program.
- start a trust for your young adult

These are some quotes I have that kept me optimistic on my journey to letting go of Trent to independent living.

"If one advances confidently in the direction of his own

dreams, and endeavors to live the life which he has imagined he will meet with a success unexpected in common hours."
—Henry David Thoreau

"What you are is what you have been, what you will be is what you do now."
—Buddha

Help People Help You

Get support, don't do it alone. Isolation is a dream killer. How do you get others to help you? First, believe that others want to help you. You can either believe people want to help you or are out to get you. I discovered I attracted others help by having a mindset that they wanted to help me. It will be easier for you if you choose the former. Being positive gave me more energy and vitality. Everyone I asked could not help but I found generally people wanted to help me succeed. I found ways to help others to help me. I made this my mantra. We all like to help others and give advice. It makes us feel good to contribute.

One way to get support is to start the process of Person Centered Planning. Pull together a selected group of individuals who have your daughter's welfare at heart. The team includes the individuals brought together to help your family and your young adult. Let go of any negative beliefs that professionals or agency representatives are out to get you. I found that whichever I chose to believe, I was right. When I believed that people wanted to help me, and I approached them in that manner, then they became open to helping me.

People want to help you succeed. My job was to provide the right information to those I asked for help. It took me years of looking for services and supports for Trent and feeling rejected to realize this. I learned to determine what it was that I really wanted to have for Trent before I asked others to help me. And I learned to be selective about what I asked for and to whom I asked.

I began to see that helping people help me began with me accepting full responsibility for achieving my goal of independent living for Trent. It also meant not asking for something Trent or I needed from someone who could not give it to me. For example, I learned not to ask for the emotional support that Trent's father could not give us. Asking for emotional support from Trent's father who was uncomfortable with that level of intimacy would have only disappointed me.

I think of the times I had support with my goals for Trent. Accepting help from my brother to purchase the house next door to his house so Trent and I could rent from him was my way of helping my brother help Trent and me. I also found support as I talked to enough people, wrote enough letters to various agencies and legislators, met with key state representatives, asked for funding, requested meetings with my State's Supported Living Council to determine what criteria was used in order that they selected the grant recipients.

As you look for ways to help others help you, consider these questions.

- Who do you feel safe with? Who can provide you with the emotional support you need?
- Who gives you support through organizations, church, entertainment, sports, or other activities?
- Who can provide financial assistance?
- Who has helped you or your young adult to this date?
- For your immediate goals, who can you ask for support and how can they help you?

How To Ask For What You Want

Here are asking tips I used that helped others help me get what I wanted to make independent living Trent's reality.

- Be clear in your own mind about what you want. Write it down. Then commit to it 500 percent. Silence the messages from others and the inner doubting negative messages that say it is not reasonable or possible.

- If you don't ASK, you don't RECEIVE. No one will ever know your interest in obtaining independent living for your young adult, if you don't assertively seek ways. It is your responsibility to make sure you get the results you desire.
- Be direct. When writing letters to state representatives or agency representatives use words such as ask, request, propose. These words say, "I'm not kidding." When language is more formal it says "I'm serious." If you must use soft words (such as I'd like, would you, could you, etc.) don't smile. Notice the difference in the feelings and intention of the stronger word choice below:

  "I request that we meet this week to discuss my son getting funds for a community coach."

  Rather than

  "I'd like to meet with you this week…" or

  "Would you meet with me this week..?"
- Set expectations. Let people know what you want them to do and sometimes by when. Again if you don't tell them, they will go on their own assumptions about what you want, which may not be what you want.

Stay Motivated

I found quotes that helped motivate me and sustained me through the process of letting go of Trent and establishing independent living. Who would have thought that a quote from one the world's greatest scientist could be applied to my life while I sought security from placing Trent into independent living.

"In the midst of difficulty lies opportunity"
—Albert Einstein.

I encountered difficulty as I became overwhelmed with the tasks of seeking independent living. I was reminded of famous people who had overcome great difficulties to achieve their dreams. It was hard for me to believe that opportunities were available for Trent. But with practice the belief became easier. That is when the opportunities and doors began to open.

Staying motivated with those tedious tasks to complete for independent living was an issue. Anxiety in the midst of it all swept over me and caused me to feel down and sometimes paralyzed. Quite often I lacked the initiative to keep moving toward our goal of independent living. Through my readings I found a quote that helped me deal with my anxiety.

"Anxiety is simply part of the condition of being human. If we were not anxious, we would never create anything."
—William Barrett

Through the anxiety, I tried to find satisfaction in just accomplishing one of the many tasks in seeking independent living while letting go of the outcome.

From the time Trent was very young to his adult years, I had the dream of independent living, but I was not sure if I wanted to just keep it as a dream or make the dream really come true for us. I continued to experience anxiety because I did not know the difference.

How about you? What is it you claim you want? Let us for a moment put aside the issues of the lack of availability of independent living programs. What would life be like if you could actually receive support and information regarding independent living? How would your life become different? Has your dream of a new and better life for your son become a burden that you carry around with you? Do you make preparations in your daughter's IEP to experience community participation and real job experience, only to discover that you really do not want to take either the risk involved in letting her live independently or the time it would take away from other parts of your life to find the supports? Are you committed to keeping your daughter with you in your home after high school?

No one is going to tell you what is right or wrong in your choices. However, make the distinction between which dream you want to keep as a dream and which you want to make become your reality. This distinction helps you to create what it is that you really want to have in your life. It lets you know which things you are willing to work for.

Try The Exercise

It will help you determine what it is that you are willing to commit.

Make a list of ten things that you want to accomplish with your family and young adult. Then prioritize them by comparing each one against the others. The benefit of this exercise is that it doesn't let you fool yourself. The order you list them in will make no difference. I will give you an example of my list when I was seeking supports and knew and understood nothing about my future.

1. Find part time work to earn enough money to have the time to search for supports needed for Trent independent living.
2. Find a community coach, roommate, and other person supports for Trent.
3. Make new friendships for myself after my divorce.
4. Establish ways to have Trent make new friends.
5. Pursue my hobby of playing the piano.
6. Play golf with my friends.
7. Write my dissertation to earn my doctorate.
8. Find a job for Trent with coworkers and a supervisor supportive of his needs.
9. Figure out financially how to make independent living our reality. Pursue affordable housing in a safe area that would meet Trent's needs.
10. Travel with friends to the beach.

I asked myself "What is more important for me today, #1 or #6, #2 or #5, #7 or #8, etc., and I checked the ones more important. I then compared 2 to 3, 2 to 4, 2 to 5, etc. then 3 to 4, 3 to 5, 3 to 6. At the end I tallied my check marks and put them in order of importance.

This is what I found.

1. Work part time and earn enough money in order to have the time to find supports for Trent. √√√√√√√
2. Find a community coach, roommate, and other person supports for Trent. √√√√√√√√
3. Make new friendships after my divorce. √√
4. Establish ways to have Trent make new friends. √√√
5. Pursue my hobby of playing the piano. √√
6. Play golf with my friends. √√
7. Write my dissertation to earn my doctorate. √√√√√
8. Find a job for Trent with coworkers and a supervisor supportive of his needs. √√√√√√
9. Figure out financially how to make independent living our reality affordable housing in a safe area that would meet Trent's needs. √√√√√√√√
10. Travel with my friends to the beach. √√√√√√√

I understood that my real commitments were to establish independent living for Trent. Playing golf and pursuing my hobby of playing the piano were not strong motivators. I even found that making new friendships could wait until after I established independent living.

Try considering these questions as you focus on daily tasks of seeking independent living for your son.

Write about an activity that will acquire supports or services for your young adult that you have been procrastinating about.

1. What are the benefits of not doing this activity? How does procrastinating serve you?

2. What would happen if you did what you have been resist-
   ing doing? What else?
3. Commit to either doing something for your young adult's
   future that you have been procrastinating about within
   the next week or not do not ever do it. Then move on.

Take Mini Steps Toward your Goal

Q: How do you eat an elephant?

A: One bite at a time.

My objective was to have independent living for Trent and
me (notice that I want to establish independent living for me,
also). I had spent years in a career as a schoolteacher. Teaching
school was not ideal for me to be able to complete the tasks to
secure independent living for Trent. I needed time during the
day to pursue the activities to acquire our independence.

Jackie's Personal Goal:

To have time to pursue all the necessary tasks to establish
independent living for Trent and have found part time consulting work that would financially support my dream.

Tasks to Complete:

1. Create my vision: I am a consultant working with adult
   agencies and/or school districts. I am compiling strategies that help transition and job placement/training for
   youth with disabilities in high schools. School districts
   and/or educators seek my services. I work out of my
   home. I appreciate the several days a week to plan and
   connect with agencies. I love being close to Trent and
   those who associate with him in order to train and follow-
   up on his activities. Trent feels warm, safe and supportive. I have a small circle of professionals, friends, and
   family who want to help Trent and me find independent
   living. I am content and happy.
2. Find consulting work to pay my basic expenses

a. Purchase a computer.

b. Make a brochure and attend conferences to market my work.

c. Network with professionals to get the word out that I am available.

3. Make Contacts for Independent Living Supports

a. Write letters to Department of Mental Retardation requesting information and assistance.

b. Write the Governor.

c. Call agencies.

d. Visit and introduce Trent to agency representatives.

e. Complete paper work for Supported Living Grant/SCL Medicaid Waiver.

f. Request others participation in Trent's behalf through Person-Centered-Planning Meetings to determine strategies for finding supports and services.

g. Network with neighbors, friends, others about work opportunities for Trent.

h. Work with supported employment agency in job development and job carving for Trent.

4. Follow-up on Networking Leads

a. Arrange to meet Jason (who is a referral from Trent's job coach) to live and assist Trent and to provide instruction to Trent in the community and live in the home.

b. Arrange for others to instruct and associate with Trent.

5. Carve Financial Support to Live Independently

a. Inquire about Subsidized Housing.

b. Complete paper work for subsidized housing and attend meetings in order to get approved.

c. Budget Trent's basic living expenses, with Supported Living Grant, monthly SSI check, and my contributions to support Trent's living arrangement.

6. Find my new Life
    a. Find an apartment for me.
    b. Find ways for me to make new friendships.
    c. Learn a new hobby.
    d. Plan to travel.

Staying motivated is a challenge to everyone who decides to create a new life. Although we are in charge of creating our new reality, it does not happen over night. We read about other families end results - not their tiresome efforts, and black days. Those who succeed do so because they hang in there through all the setbacks while staying focused on their goals. I mainly stayed motivated by enlisting support from others and taking care of Trent and myself. I persisted because I loved what I was trying to accomplish for Trent and me. I could not think of any other way that we were willing to live our lives.

Some times I would let myself get depressed or get the blues. These are some strategies I found that helped me.

Strategies for Coping with the Blues:

1. Be sad, depressed, or even grumpy. I gave myself a time limit of an hour, a day, or a week. For a limited period only, I allowed myself to be sad or depressed. During that time I did not have to pretend everything was OK or even humor others. I simply gave myself permission to be completely miserable. However, at the end of the period, I stopped. At that time, I moved forward with my efforts. It may help to tell your family that you will be allowing yourself to go through a down period so they can support you too.
2. Exercise. I found that physical exercise increased my vitality. The kind of exercise whatever your choice, increases endorphins and diminishes depression and emotional upsets.
3. Keep a journal. I found this approach extremely valuable. By writing down my feelings, tasks I have done or need to do, my expectations, what I wish would happen, what is working, and

most importantly my prayers, I found relief, answers, and validation on the work I had accomplished. I found that I could have a great dialogue with myself in my journal.

4. Practice compassion-with yourself. I sought ways to be patient about my progress I made toward achieving my dreams of independent living for Trent. I realized that things take time.

5. Do something practical. Anything! Choose a small task. Complete it. Then show someone what you did. Showing another person your accomplishment is important because you will experience both the success and the validation of that success.

6. Honor your body. Eat only foods that are good for you, and are wonderfully prepared. They will increase your vitality.

7. Listen to motivational tapes or read motivating books. When I was feeling depressed and paralyzed, I discovered that this strategy pulled me out of my slump period. The tips helped and I felt that I had a friend cheering me on.

8. Find a way to give yourself a daily reward. Write down all the things that bring you joy. I would choose one from the list to give back to myself everyday.

Helping Trent Become Self - Determined

It has been always been my focus to find interventions that would empower Trent to increase his self - determined behavior. Hayden & Abery (1994) define personal self - determination as being able to affirm one's personhood through choice, self - representation, and empowerment. Developing skills in areas of independence, choice making, self - management, problem solving and opportunities to use them are fundamental to membership in society.

I discovered through trial and error ways that helped Trent. During times of change or increased stress, Trent needed a clear understanding from the expectations of others who supported him and why he needed to exhibit certain behaviors. Part 4 of this book discusses strategies used that helped Trent increase his self - determined behavior.

In the past, three strategies have been successful in helping Trent understand the unknown, in new situations and new people. These strategies included reading a short book about the particular situation, writing a social story, and/or making and reading visual supports (i.e. check lists).

Shortly after Trent graduated, when Trent's father and I separated, it was difficult for Trent to understand why his parents were apart. Trent became confused. He exhibited sadness and some behaviors that were evident to me that he needed to know what was happening, why it was happening and how he would be affected. I thought if I could find a particular book that provided helpful information to children about divorce, he might begin to accept our new circumstances.

I searched bookstores for children's books that would help explain to Trent how to accept and live with divorce of parents. Unfortunately these books addressed divorce for the young child as the audience. Although these books were inappropriate for Trent age, I found one book with cartoon characters - which I thought was better than a book with real pictures of small children. It seemed to work as an age appropriate book, because even adults read cartoon scripts in the newspaper.

Trent needed visual supports that encouraged his acceptance to new community experiences and new people. So Trent and I pulled out the markers, paper, and scissors and made visual supports. Picture schedules, written checklists, and structured routines were the supports that he required in order to help him feel safe in his new life.

After I organized the sections for his personal notebook, I realized the approaches used to help Trent's adaptations to his new environments and new life could also benefit other families who were seeking solutions for handling the challenges within one's family with their young adult with autism. I believed if I included information about how Trent as a full participant helped himself, it could benefit not only families living with autism but also those individuals who associate with and support our young adults with autism who are going through the transition years to adulthood.

Most importantly, the people associating and supporting Trent needed to have general ways to communicate and relate to him as an individual with autism. I knew if Trent were to participate successfully in leisure and job opportunities in the community, he would require natural supports from others. Trent's job coach and community coach facilitated the natural supports in various settings Trent participated. What approaches were used? We shared our insights and determined the supports that would benefit Trent as he was working and participating in leisure activities within the community.

People who may benefit from reading this book include those who associate and support young adults with autism. These individuals may be paid support people such as a community coach. They may also include people who associate naturally with the individual having autism throughout the community. Some people who are targets for natural supports include: peers, coworkers, employers, community coaches, and neighbors. Because these support people are not likely to have backgrounds in education, speech therapy, psychology, counseling, etc., general strategies need to be offered to assist the natural support in practical ways regarding how to associate and communicate with the young adult having autism.

I knew if I could interpret Trent's behaviors and his responses to certain stimuli and situations, and express in writing that interpretation indicating ways that help meet Trent's adaptations to his environment, then others would understand Trent's needs a little more. Most importantly, if others who associated with Trent understood how to support Trent and applied these strategies, then Trent would reap the benefits of having his needs met. As Trent worked and participated in community environments with others while applying the supports he required, his community coaches or coworkers were enhancing Trent's chances for community access and community success.

It is very important to understand that the general strategies in this book that worked for Trent may or may not work for every young adult. These are general strategies drawn from the literature and based on general and positive responses. It is my belief that as the general public observes community coaches, employees, neighbors, and friends responding positively to individuals with autism, than positive perceptions are planted like a seed. Hopefully after years those perceptions may continue to grow toward accepting individuals with autism in the community. If others can get to the point of understanding that individuals with autism have require certain supports to be included, then acceptance begins. Positive perceptions by the community toward individuals with autism are critical to their acceptance while participating in the community.

Educating the Community

Trent and other adult individuals with autism face extreme challenges as they approach adulthood and are introduced to new people and new situations. Based on my personal experience as a mother and an educator, I found that when a traditional approach fails to work for the young adult with autism, the perception from others is that the problem lies within that individual with autism. Some professionals view the individual having a disability as the source of his/her problems. I believe that there has been a failure from professionals and support personnel to properly determine the supports needed to enhance the autistic person's success in the community.

When Trent exhibited occasional inappropriate behavior, it saddened me that others saw only his behavior and missed seeing the person inside. His need for friendship, to belong to a group, or desire to work on a job may all go unrecognized, if perceptions were less than supportive.

It is my belief that when others label individuals with autism based on their behavior rather than understanding their basic human needs, negative perceptions can become the greatest barrier for inclusion. It is my hope that the book will diminish such negativity and shed light in meaningful ways: 1). The family must have a focused perspective in order to complete the tasks so independent living can be reached for a young adult and 2). others who associate with families and individuals with autism will understand more clearly the supports necessary for the young adult and his family as they make the transition into independent living.

Part Four

TRENT'S MESSAGE

All supports listed in this book are general approaches that are known to be successful with other adults having autism. Trent is not a savant. He has autism. Through out the years we have tried various alternative therapies and none have proven to help Trent. The strategies that help Trent are general and may apply to other individuals with autism who exhibit similar behaviors. However, it must be noted that each person having autism is an individual and the results of a behavior functional assessment should be considered in order to determine the appropriate supports needed.

As you read the following pages, note that the rest of the book is written as Trent's message presented to the reader in first person. Trent relates his feelings, desires, and needs to me on a daily basis. The interpretation is mine based on my understanding of how to relate and help Trent. Trent has fully participated in the development of this book. We continue to work together to open his future to the quality of life that many of us enjoy.

HOW YOU CAN HELP ME

Create My Environment

- Create a structured, ordered environment
  If the environment is inviting it will provide me the opportunity for building success and trust.

- Create an environment that meets my sensory needs
  Demonstrate to others who are around me ways to talk to me and help me when I become confused or experience change.

- Create an environment where the expectations are clear to me

- Create an environment that encourages me to become independent. I am learning to be come less dependent on others. When I learn steps toward helping myself, I am becoming more independent.

- Create an environment where everyone works together as a team.

Ways You Can Talk With Me

It helps me if you know how to talk to me and give me information or just being social with me. Here are some ways that help me:

Please talk to me using words and sentences that are simple and to the point. At times, I can understand a portion of the words spoken to me. Please be clear. I may get confused and frustrated when you use too many directions and elaborations.

For example, at work you may say to me, "Put on your gloves, get the cleaner, and go to the locker room".

Sometimes even this statement may be too confusing. I may have only heard the last request, which was go to the locker room. You may have to break your direction down more for me.

90

Try saying this to me.

> "It is time to go to the locker room. Put on your gloves."
> When we are in the locker room and I have my gloves on, say, "get the cleaner".

Please use a positive tone when talking with me. I can sense by your tone if you are upset with me. In fact, if you are upset, I may get confused and may actually do the opposite of what you intended for me to do.

Please tell me what tasks I am doing well. I then begin to understand more clearly what it is that I am doing is considered appropriate. Please ignore some things I do that do not matter much.

For example, in new settings there are many different things that I am learning to tolerate and understand. It is helpful if you break down my task so I am working on a few skills that are most important for me to succeed.

I may have to visit a new grocery store that is different from the familiar store. I am being challenged to search for items on a shelf at the grocery store while at the same time reading the signs on the aisles.

Please do not require me to read a grocery list and search for the items on the shelf to place in the cart. It may be too over-whelming for me to work on both tasks. Choose one task or ask me to choose which task I would prefer to do.

When you are explaining something to me, or when you see me doing something I should not do, try not to use words "No or Don't". These words make me think you are mad at me or I did something wrong.

For example, if I reached for a can of peas and I missed understanding the request you made to retrieve a can of green beans from the shelf, please do not say, "No, Trent, pick up the can of green beans."

Your correction may further confuse because your direction included the word no.

Tell me in words that help me change what I am doing. When you give me praise, please be clear.

For example, say to me, " Trent, you folded all the towels, or Trent you placed the towels correctly in the closet." I can understand these statements better than if you say, "Trent, you are working good today".

Meeting New People

When you introduce someone new to me, I may not always look at the new person. But I always like to be included when new people are around. I have learned to shake hands well when I first meet someone. I always like it:

- when you tell the new person my name and I learn his name.

- when the new person walks over to me and offers his or her hand first.

- when you invite me to join your group even though at first I do not appear that I want to. Sometimes I enjoy a new experience even though I may only partially participate.

Recreation

I enjoy bowling. My community coach takes me to different places on Saturdays.

I like to bowl on the bowling team at Special Olympics. I have made new friends. Belonging to a team makes me feel accepted.

I may not always participate fully in an activity as others do. Please don't let that keep you from inviting me to be with others. Because once I am in a situation with others, I enjoy being part of a group.

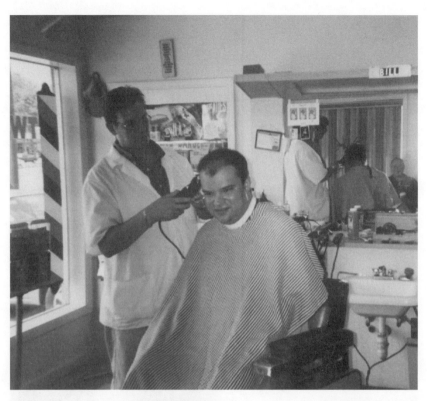

I like getting my hair cut.

I enjoy music. I am attending a bluegrass music festival outside Heine Brothers Coffee shop on a warm summer evening.

One of my favorite past times is shopping at the mall for new clothes. One brand I really like is NIKE. I also like bright colors such as orange and yellow. I spend my paycheck on my clothes.

I like to wash my mother's car.

I like riding my bike. I have another person ride with me. I am working on stopping at the stop signs and waiting for cars to past by.

I like being with my brothers. I visit my brother Todd at his apartment. Todd invited me over for dinner.

I have learned to order my food at McDonalds.

Jason and I occasionally eat dinner out in nice restaurants. We are eating at Wick's Pizza. At first the loud music and noise bothered me. Now I enjoy eating at Wick's and watching all the people around.

Exercising at the YMCA

I like walking on the treadmill at the YMCA. When I exercise, I like to turn the machine on for exactly 60 minutes. I do not stop until 60 minutes is finished.

At the YMCA, I look around and see other people working out. I see that I can be part of a group. I like working out like others do.

At first I did not want to exercise. But I am learning that exercise helps me feel better. Going to the YMCA is an activity I can do everyday and it is a club I can belong to.

Going to the Library

I enjoy playing games on the computer at the Public Library.

My community coach took me to the library every Wednesday.

Going to the Zoo

I enjoy walking around at the zoo and being outside.

Gardening

One of my chores at my house is to keep the flowers watered. I have learned that I am responsible for certain chores at my house.

I also help my grandmother with the yard work. I can help trim the grass off the sidewalk, cut grass with a push mower, and clip the bushes.

Cooking

I enjoy cooking differ-ent dishes in the kitchen. My favorite dish to prepare is lazagna. I especially enjoy sprinkling the cheese and pouring the sauce over the noodles.

Laundry

I have learned to wash my own clothes.

I like to wash my clothes at night after I take my shower.

Sometimes I have diffi-culty pouring the right amount in the machine. I may pour too much or not enough. You may want to continue supporting me in determining appropriate amounts.

How To Introduce Me to a New Environment and to Help Me Adapt to a New Situation

I often refuse to go to new places or do new activities and tasks. I am unsure because I don't know what to expect. Sometimes a lot of new people, sounds, and movement occur in a situation. At times I become agitated or frustrated. So I may need to get used to the environment slowly. As I become more familiar with the task or environment, I usually accept the environment.

It helps me when you prepare me for new things and places by using one of these methods:

- help me write a social story about the new situation
- use pictures
- take me in the car to do a drive by visit to the new place. The first time do not require that I get out and go in if I am feeling unsure.

I may accept a new situation following my first short visit.

For Example:

When my mother got married, I escorted her down the aisle during the ceremony. Three days before the wedding, my community coach, my mother and I visited the chapel. I listened to the music, practiced walking my mother down the aisle, sat in the pew, looked around the chapel, and got use to the

Travis, Todd and Trent

surroundings. When the big night came, I was ready to walk mom down the aisle even with all the people watching me.

My brothers were proud of me as I participated in mom's wedding.

Please try these strategies when you are introducing me to new environments when I cannot have a short visit before.

• Use pictures or a written checklist to explain to me what will happen.

When I am in a new environment and you notice I am beginning to get upset take me out of the situation briefly. I do not want to get upset in front of other people. I could leave shortly and then come back later. I may just need a little time to get use to the new situation. When I have the appropriate behavior in the new environment, please tell me I have handled the situation well.

Teach Me to Attend to You
When You Speak to Me

When I hear many directions and lots of words, I may not understand, so I may not listen.

Example 1

If a coworker says, " We will go to the storage room when you show me you are ready." This directive may be unclear for me. I need more information.

For example, try to be concise and clear. A coworker at Kmart may ask me to follow him to another area to work. It could help me if you tried doing these things.

• First, make sure you have my attention.

• Then say, "Trent, follow me to the storage room" accompanied by a gesture (especially if it is new to me).

It helps me if you first know in your mind what you want me to do. In addition, know why it is you want me to do a particular task.

Example 2

If I am asked to clean out the lockers, please do not say, "Dust all the lockers." This tells me what to do, but does not tell specifically how well I must work.

Instead, if you provide me with a list of the number of lockers and a cloth to wipe them out, I will understand the purpose of the task. Also, please model for me the task that I am suppose to learn. You have now made it clearer for me and I know what to expect.

Help Me Understand My Feelings

You can help me best understand my feelings by helping me label my feelings.

I also have great difficulty understanding your feelings and

I have great difficulty expressing my feelings. Those supporting me can help me label feelings in natural situations.

If you can place a name of the feeling along with a possible reason for why I may be having the feeling, then it may help me understand my feelings better.

Some Examples:

"I'm mad. Travis is wearing my new shirt."

"I'm happy. I am watching jeopardy."

"Buying a new Nike shirt at Footlocker makes me happy."

"Dad is not home this weekend, I can not go to his house. I feel sad that I cannot visit my dad."

Changing My Routine:

When I started my new job, I had to get used to a new routine. Because of this change of working at my new job, I had not been going to the YMCA for exercise as much. Exercising at the YMCA had been an activity I enjoyed - especially walking on the treadmill. So for a short time, my focus was getting use to working at my job and exercise was taken out of my routine.

So when my community coach asked if I wanted to go back to the YMCA, I strongly replied, "NO." The YMCA had not been part of my routine for over a month, so I rejected going. Each day I responded with a strong "NO" and refused to even get out of the car when my community coach drove me to the YMCA.

Mom encouraged me day after day to try the YMCA again. We wrote several social stories and my uncle and grandma reminded me to go into the YMCA before I left in the car with my community coach. Still I refused to go.

The next day my mom suggested that I just try exercising again. I got into the car, but before I left our house I was so mad I ripped my shirt. I did not want to leave my afternoon cartoon shows. But mom said all I had to do was just walk into the YMCA and find the treadmill - then I could leave. I felt better about just visiting and not staying very long.

When we arrived, I did not want to get out of the car. Mom handed me money for the parking meter. This helped me redirect my thinking. After I placed the money into the meter, I went into the YMCA. We took the elevator to the 4th floor. I found the treadmill and walked on it for one minute. Afterwards, I walked over to mom and said, "time for going home."

Mom reminded me that I did what I was asked to do. She explained to me that I have choices to make and when I follow through with these choices in a cooperative, calm way, I am making good choices. She reminds me that when I choose to be cooperative even when I do not want to, I am becoming more and more independent everyday.

The very next day my community coach drove me to the YMCA. I exercised on the treadmill for exactly 60 minutes.

I am learning that my activities may change every now and then. With each new situation I encounter, I have choices and I must follow through with my choices. When others who support me point out to me my small successes, this helps me understand that I am making right choices. To others I may seem difficult and obnoxious. But please know that my routine helps me make sense of my world. I can adapt but I need time and I need others to be patient and understanding.

Help Me Handle Changes in my Work Environment:

Give me enough information. Tell me first what is going to happen then what will happen afterwards. If there are changes, tell me and please include me and with the plans.

For example: If I am going to learn a new work task at my job, it may help me if you prepare me for it the day before. Take

me to the area I will work. Show me the materials and demonstrate the task for me. Tell me that when I come into work
tomorrow I will need to work in this area.

Offer me help when I need it. I feel much more secure if I
know who I can get help from. Include me in the work plans.
This makes me feel part of the plan and I will adapt better to the
change.

Remember please tell me what will happen and how you
expect me to react. Remember when you use pictures or written
words I understand so much more.

Waiting is Sometimes Difficult for Me

Sometimes I have to wait. I am ready to go to work. I am
waiting for the Tarc 3 bus. Sometimes I have to wait even when
I do not want to. I am learning that there are times the bus will
be late. I am choosing to wait calmly.

What you can do to help me:
• As I sit patiently, remind me that I am waiting patiently. Help
  me understand that the bus may be late sometimes and when
  I accept leaving late tell me how well I accepted this change.

Interventions That Help Me Build My Self-Determined Behavior

1. Schedule to Keep
    If I have a say in choosing an activity I may participate
    more willingly. For example, you may offer me a choice
    of going to a movie, walking in the park, or going to the
    Mall and getting a haircut. If I can choose the activity
    and then I am likely to choose appropriate behavior. I
    also, feel that I have some control in what I do in my free
    time.

2. Make it easy for me to see a link between a goal I have set for myself and a choice I have made.

For example, if I am working on getting ready on time in the morning for work. You might say to me, "Trent you made a point last night of choosing your clothes and placing them out for your morning shower. Today I see you are ready and on time.

Or, if I am having difficulty staying on task at work, you can make me a goal card. The card helps me stay focused. I sometimes get stuck (obsess) on objects at work. If you encourage me to look at my goal card as a reminder of the focus I am suppose to have, this helps me. Also, if you remind I am following through according to the goal, then I can see the link between my goal and my choices.

3. Assist me in asking for help when I need it.

Provide me guidance in understanding consequences of my choices.

Write the problem at the top of the paper. List for me the choices I can make and help me label whether each choice will be 'appropriate behavior' or 'NOT appropriate behavior'.

Provide me with opportunities to brainstorm choices.

For example, if I have several hours before I need to leave for a movie or to the YMCA, what are my choices of things I could do? Play CD's, Help Grandma cook, wash dishes?

4. Provide me with opportunities to self-evaluate my performance in working on a particular task. Point out what I've done that's like the model.

For example, Jason said, "Look you raked the leaves in your area of the yard just as I did in my area. Do you see any leaves left on the ground that you missed?" If so, what do you need to do now?

5. Ask me directive questions so that I can compare my readiness for participating in the activity.

    For example, say, "Do you have your wallet and key?" "I'll know you are ready to leave after you get your wallet and key." Please say these phrases to me, "Are you ready to go into the grocery store?" I'll know you are ready when you say, "go to store" or say, "ready."

6. Ask me to consider choices I've made in the recent past and the consequences of those choices. It has helped me to write down the choices I made and to write down the choice I could have made. Writing them down helps me distinguish from the two choices. This will remind me choices I need to consider when I am faced with a difficult situation.

7. Help me set simple goals and help me check to see if I am reaching them.

    For example, say this to me, "Trent, you have shown me that you want to cut the grass. Let's make a list of the steps we need to cut the grass."

    (1). Walk to the garage and get the push mower.

    (2). Push the mower in the front yard.

    (3). Look for any grass you may have missed.

    (4). Push the mower back over the taller areas of grass.

Waking In the Morning

It is hard for me because I do not like to get up early.

One of my goals is to get up with an alarm clock and without being called.

Before I lived independently it helped when mom called upstairs and said "You have 5 more minutes". When I was given 5 more minutes, I had time to process the information. After the 5 minutes was up, I was prepared to get up.

I now live with my roommate. So I have two alarm clocks.

My family reminds me that when I get up by myself, I am becoming more and more independent. I am working on becoming more independent.

Through out the day when my family catches me doing an activity or a chore with less dependence, they remind me how well I am doing. They often say to me, "Trent you are becoming more and more independent everyday."

I am being encouraged to remind myself, "I am living independently."

Sometimes when others point out my independent behavior, it helps me recognize what independence looks like even in small meaningful activities.

Challenging the Obsession with My Clothes

I am more comfortable with certain kinds of clothes or wearing my clothes a certain way. Sometimes my clothes bother me. I am learning to tell the person I am with.

First, I like to cut all my tags off my shirts. The tags bother me.

Second, it is hard for me to change into a new season of clothing. When I must change to fall and winter clothes after I wear shorts all summer, I have to adapt. I like to wear loose fitting underware with my shorts.

But when summer turns to autumn and the weather is cooler, I like to wear short underwear called briefs when I wear long pants everyday. If I wear loose underware with long pants, I developed an obsession with going into the bathroom wanting to smooth the bulky material under my long pants.

So my mother suggested that I wear short underware (briefs) in the fall and winter with my long pants.

When my clothes bother me I can say "clothes" or point to a picture in my notebook and the person with me can help me.

Third, I need to know when it is necessary to wear special dress up clothes to special places. I have a sports jacket, nice shirts, pants, and nice shoes. So it helps me if I know ahead of time when I need to where these special clothes.

Places I may wear special clothes is to Sunday School, Church, Holidays, or when I go out to eat at a restaurant at a special time.

Lastly, I do not like my socks to get all stretched out. Stretched out socks get all bulky and gathered up in my shoe. I have developed an obsession with taking my shoes off and on trying to perfectly smooth out the material of my socks. When I have newer socks to wear, I put my socks and shoes on only one time. Sometimes when I get real frustrated, it is hard for me to move on to the next activity in a cooperative way.

My TV Shows

I like to have my activities occur at the same time everyday. I used to have my routine built around all my TV shows. I learned that it is not possible to have everyday look the same. I used to know the time every T.V. show came on and the station it was on. I did not like to miss even one T.V. show during the afternoon and evening. Sometimes I have gotten really mad and upset when my family made stop watching TV to go on an outing.

My community coach and mom worked with me to break this habit. They were patient with me as they encouraged me to leave for short periods.

When I meet the goal of leaving for even an hour, I have had another successful experience.   Each time I had a successful experience, they reminded me that I was accepting new experiences that helped me become more independent.

My family says sometimes my day needs to change. I am working on going out of the house at different times to do other activities.

I am working on going out of the house at different time to do other activities. Some activities I participate in with my community coach or family:

- Getting a hair cut
- Attending a music festival
- Shopping at the Mall
- Washing the car
- Riding my bike
- Visiting my brother Todd
- Dine in a restaurant

Others who do not understand my challenges may say I am demanding and selfish. Please know this. I want people around me to understand I have difficulty experiencing the world from your eyes.

This is what you can do to help me

- Help me develop new activities slowly.
- Offer me a variety of choices, for example either a walk in the park, or dine out in a restaurant.
- Provide me with a chart that could help me understand what time my favorite T.V. shows are on. With a chart, when I had to miss a show to participate in an activity I placed card with the name of the activity over the T.V. show on the chart.

This helped me understand how long I would be away from home. I am learning to do new activities outside of my house.

Look at the example of a list of TV shows.
T.V. Daily Shows

Time	Name of Show
2:30	Magic School Bus
3:00	Power Rangers
3:30	Beast Wars
4:00	Digimon Digital Monsters
4:30	Power Rangers Lost Galaxy
5:00	Home Improvement

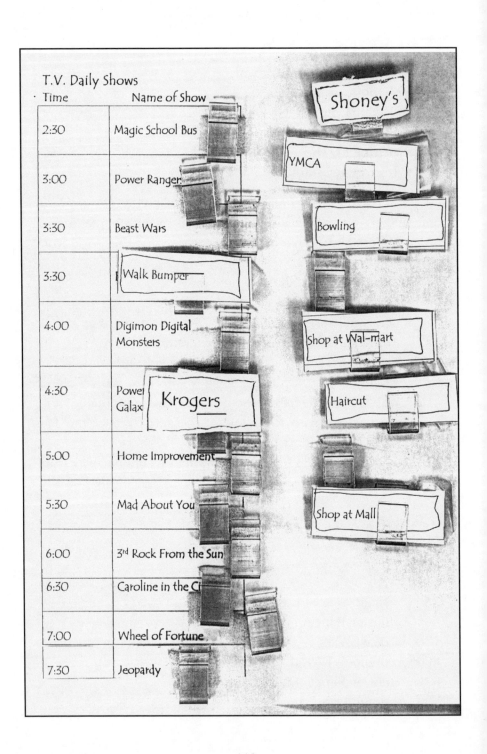

T.V. Daily Shows

Time	Name of Show
2:30	Magic School Bus
3:00	Power Rangers
3:30	Beast Wars
3:30	Walk Bumper
4:00	Digimon Digital Monsters
4:30	Power Galax
5:00	Home Improvement
5:30	Mad About You
6:00	3rd Rock From the Sun
6:30	Caroline in the City
7:00	Wheel of Fortune
7:30	Jeopardy

Shoney's

YMCA

Bowling

Shop at Wal-mart

Krogers

Haircut

Shop at Mall

My Vocalizations

When I am tired I may get agitated or grumpy. I may start to make noises (vocalizations) that may indicate one of several possibilities. I may be overloaded by all the sensations around me or I may be fascinated and interested by the sights and sounds of the environment, or I am just simply tired. These noises are a sign to others that I am having difficulty coping. If I become tired or need help, I am learning to tell the person I am with how I feel. For example, I can say "I feel tired" or I could point to a picture in my notebook of a bed.

Sometimes I make noises (vocalizations) and withdraw from my environment. I usually withdraw only when I am at home, and when I am transferring from one activity to the next. I usually need only 15 minutes. I have learned that when I withdraw, the time is helpful for me to get ready for the next activity.

So if you see me withdrawing into my own world for a short time and if it is not important I participate, don't try to stop me. Please allow me this time.

Getting Frustrated:

Sometimes I would get frustrated when my family made changes in the house. For example, I did not like our furniture or other items changed around.

1. I did not like it when the furniture was moved around. I like everything the same way.

   Sometimes I do not get my way. I am still learning that I have to get used to new furniture and moving old items away. It may seem to you that I am a pain to be around, but you can help me accept new things by being patient. Also, you may need to be firm with me, insisting the furniture or items must stay the way you place it.

2. When I left the house for an outing, I liked to make sure I completed certain actions. At times I have followed a

ritual. It helped me close a part of my day or an activity when I followed a pattern.

For example, when I left my house in the morning I turned off a light, turned other lights on, closed a blind, placed the toilet seat in a down position, and lastly turned the T.V. on channel 9.

Others may call me obsessive/compulsive and may think I am a major problem person to be around. But you can help me help myself. Please know that when I place items in a certain order, that order helped me to cope. Most importantly, please know that I have difficulty understanding what others may need at that time. Often times I may need someone to be patient and consistent with me in redirecting me away from the ritual behaviors.

Help Me Understand Your Intention

Please do not yell at me or give me threats to correct my behavior. I do not understand your intention. I will likely get more confused and upset not understanding why you speak to me so harshly. I may become so upset that I will not know how to do what you are asking of me.

These are examples of statements I may not know how to respond.
- "You know better than that," or
- "I've told you before not to walk around the store without asking."

Please say to me,
- "I expect you to walk with me and shop with me."
- Or say,"First, ask, "I want to get cereal" before you walk away from me. Then tell me, "OK, go to another aisle and get your favorite cereal."

Speaking Harshly or Vague

When someone speaks harshly to me I will probably not do what you want me to do.

When someone uses words that are vague, I may become confused.

For example if you say "If you don't get your money, then you can't go to McDonalds." This statement may confuse me.

It is better to say to me, "Get your money out. Then we will go to McDonalds." This statement tells me what to do.

Encourage Me

Encourage me to choose appropriate behavior by speaking clearly to me.

Tell me what to do. Please do not mention what not to do. For example, "If I pick up an object off the floor and put it in my mouth, say, "Put it in the trash can." Or offer your hand and say, "Give it to me".

If you say, "don't put it in your mouth", I will probably put it in my mouth because I may not hear don't and may only "here put it in my mouth."

If I am at work and I grab a bag or chair from one of the customers that does not belong to me, please say, " Put the bag back or Put the chair back." Please do not say, "You must not grab the bag or chair." I may only hear grab the bag.

Please choose your statements carefully when you are training me.

Positive statements tell me the behavior you want from me. Where as, the negative statements do not provide me with the information about what to do appropriately or different.

Your tone of voice, or facial expression may confuse me and change the meaning of a question, or direction. When you give me a direction, tell me what needs to be done. Please do not challenge me. I may become defensive or upset.

In fact I may do the opposite of what is asked when directions are given in a threatening manner.

I have heard people say that I am stubborn or I just want attention. I want others to know that I am trying, but there may be several reasons for my behavior.

- I may need time to process what you have said or I need time to get use to the environment.
- I may be confused and unsure about what is going to happen to me next.
- I may want to have a choice about my activities.
- I become fixated on new things to look at in my environment and I may have difficulty moving from one activity to the next.

For example, if I become obsessed with an object at work or arrange a stick on the sidewalk and I refuse to follow your direction to move on, please gently guide me and say, "It's time to go home". "Please do not say in a loud, strong voice, "You must go home right now!"

Sometimes it helps to ask me questions to get me focused. For example, "Where are you supposed to be?" or "What are you supposed to be doing?" can help me correct my behavior if you are speaking to me in a neutral tone.

A Problem Solving Activity

I have a chart that I have used with my mom to help me understand the consequences of my choices. Also, it helped me understand options I may want to think about next time.

Problem Solving Chart

Problem_____

_____

_____

_____

_____

Choice#1

_____

_____

_____Appropriate_____NOT Appropriate_____

Choice #2

_____

_____

_____Appropriate_____NOT Appropriate_____

Choice #3

_____

_____

_____Appropriate_____NOT Appropriate_____

What I Learned To Do About Anger

I don't get angry often now. But when I did get angry, I felt so overwhelmed and afraid I did not know what to do. I was learning to cope with my angry feelings. Some of the angry behaviors I had included: hitting my head with my hands or ripping my shirt. One of the ways I have learned to work on controlling my anger:

I say the word GENTLE and I practice GENTLE HANDS by touching arm softly at times when I am calm. I also say the word 'CALM' over and over quietly and softly.

My mom and grandmother say that everyone feels anger sometimes. But they also tell me anger can be dangerous. I know very well it's not OK to hurt people, things, or even myself when I feel angry.

I am learning there are safe ways to make myself feel better.

Mom has provided me with a small card to carry in my wallet to remind me of the steps I can take to control my anger. I am learning that I have choices to make. I can choose to be angry or I can choose ways to try and stay calm.

I have learned to have gentle hands. When I get upset, it helps me if you remind me to have gentle hands.

Angry Feelings Checklist

Sometimes it helped me when I made a list of things that made me angry. I learned to label the things that made me feel angry. I may not have the ability to tell someone that I have an angry feeling, because I become confused. I started a list of events or reasons that occurred before I expressed my anger. This list helped me to label possible reasons I got angry.

___Having too many new different places to visit

___Having too many new activities to do in one day

___Missing My Dad

___Missing my Brother Todd

___Not getting to watch every T.V. Show I want

___When People hurry me.

___When people are angry toward me or another person

___Having too many new people to meet at one time

Ways I Learned How To Work Through My Anger

- Breathe Deeply
- Repeat the words "calm" and "be gentle"
- Tell others how I feel by pointing to feeling pictures.
- Find a safe place to be alone.
- Light touch my finger tips
- Eat a mint
- Hold a checklist in my pocket of what I can expect to happen on my outing.

I used this activity when I talked with my mother. I liked to write down what we talked about.

Ways I know my family cares about me:

_____

_____

Ways I know I am important:

_____

_____

Ways I am a special person:

_____

_____

Ways I can feel happy:

_____

_____

Examples that show I can do many things well:_____

_____

_____

Ways I know my Dad loves me:_____

_____

_____

Ways I know my Mom loves me:_____ _____

_____

_____

Ways I know Todd and Travis cares about me:_____

_____

_____

Ways I know my Grandma cares about me:_____

_____

_____

Ways I know Uncle Craig cares about me:_____

_____

_____

Ways that show I am accepting changes in my family:_____

_____

_____

Ways I show I love both of my parents:_____

_____

Thinking Good Thoughts

My family tells me it is important to think good thoughts. My thoughts will help me become more positive with others and in new places.

I like to check off these thoughts as I read them out loud and as a family member helps me complete each sentence.

___ I know my family cares about me because:

___ I know I am important person because:

___ I am a special Person because:

___ I know I am happy when:

___ I can do many things well such as:

___ I know my Dad is proud of me when:

___ I know my Mom is proud of me when:

___ I know Todd and Travis care about me when they:

___ I know my Grandma loves cares about me when she:

___ I know Uncle Craig enjoys listening to music and watching baseball on TV with me.

___ I can accept changes in my family.

___ I love both of my parents.

___ I am becoming more and more independent everyday.

___ I choose to be a gentleman.

___ I am working on making good choices.

Checklist for Evaluating my Environment

This is a checklist so others can determine if the job, event, or activity is a good place for me.

Is my independence being encouraged?	Yes	No
Are other people around me working together?	Yes	No
Is the environment able to meet my needs?	Yes	No
Do I have visual supports that help me understand the tasks I have to do?	Yes	No
Can others be flexible with me?	Yes	No
If there is a problem in my environment, can changes be made to help me become more successful?	Yes	No

I Need Your Patience
(An Analogy)

Please be patient as you encourage me to enter new unfamiliar territory. Sometimes facing a new unfamiliar environment is like getting into a very cold swimming pool or lake.

I am frightened, and insecure about the cold water. I walk toward the water and just stand - observing. You encourage me to test the water by just placing my foot into the water. For a long time I ignore your wishes and I refuse to enter the water. If you force me to enter, I reject by screaming. I must choose when to enter and at my own pace. But most importantly I need you to be patient with me and to encourage me to try new cold water.

I choose to put my foot in the water testing the temperature to see how cold and safe it is. The water is cold, I am afraid to go in. After much encouragement from you and as time passes, I choose to enter slowly so my body can get adjusted to the temperature. I choose to stay briefly, and quickly move out of the water. I am not ready yet. I need you to support my choice. Please tell me I can try again later.

If you are patient with me, I will try again. I walk slowly and place my foot carefully in the water. Entering in slowly, I take my time getting use to the water. After a short experience in the water, I choose to get out of the pool again. I have a setback. Please do not give up. I will try again later. Remember I need the comfort of knowing that you support my choice to wait until I am ready to move again into the cold water of my new life.

I try again. The water is cold and does not feel comfortable yet. However, this time I notice the water is not as scary as before and actually becomes more tolerable as I stay. In fact, the water is comfortable. I begin to play in my own way in the water. I have accepted the cold water.

As I enter the cold waters of my life I take one more step toward learning self - determination. Thank you for encouraging me and being patient as I choose to move forward into my new unfamiliar life.

Without Words

When I sing and rock to the beat, I appreciate the language of music.

When I exhibit reverence in church, I respect spirituality.

When I join a group, I may only partially participate, but I like belonging.

When I earn money at my job or for a chore and choose to spend my money on a new shirt, I am developing my self-determination.

When I choose a movie to attend, I enjoy recreation just as others do.

When I leave my house eagerly for work, I seek a reason to get up everyday.

When I walk with a spring at my job, I am exhibiting pride and value work.

When I enjoy visits and family get-togethers, I feel connected and safe.

My quality of life is dependent upon you

As you extend your patience and effort to help me belong to a world I have difficulty understanding,

you affect my happiness,

you affect my life.

Please do not give up on me.

—Jackie Altman Marquete

Glossary of Terms

Activity center: A daily program for adults with disabilities to participate in activities that teaches community and vocational skills.

Adaptive behavior: An individual's capability to apply acquired skills to new environments, tasks, and people.

Adult day programs: A daily program where adults with disabilities participate in activities that emphasize training in daily living skills, social skills, recreational skills, and prevocational skills.

Advocacy: To act or speak out on the behalf of another individual or a group in order to promote change.

Advocate: A person who speaks in the behalf of another individual or group to promote change.

Community participation: An individual's expansion of opportunities within the community into roles valued by the community.

Competitive employment: Part - time or full - time jobs offering wages at the going rate in the open labor market.

Developmental Disability (DD): A severe mental or physical disability that significantly impacts a person's activities that require the person to depend on life long care and treatment.

Employability skills: Personal traits and habits such as dependability, that are necessary for successful employment; sometimes called "work adjustment skills."

Expressive language: Communication through speech, writing, augmentative communication, or gestures.

Habilitation: Training for specific skills and abilities (e.g., dressing, eating, maneuvering a wheel chair) in order that the individual become independent as possible.

Inclusion: Providing necessary supports and services so that the adults with disabilities can participate with other adults who do not have disabilities in the community, and recreation activities.

Independent living skills: Basic skills needed by people with disabilities to function with as little help as possible. Examples of skills include self - help (e.g. bathing, dressing), housekeeping, community living (e.g. shopping, using public transportation) etc.

Individual Education Program (IEP): A written plan for each student in special education describing the student's present levels of performance, annual goals, including short term objectives, specific special education and related services, dates for beginning and duration of services, and the method in which the IEP will be evaluated.

Job coach: A professional providing job development, training and support to the employee with a disability. Some supports for the employee include: increasing job skills, interpersonal relations, and any other job related needs.

Medicaid: A federal state, program that provides medical services primarily to individuals with low incomes.

Natural homes: Places that are generally thought of a dwellings for people, such as apartments, houses, townhouses, trailers, etc.

Natural supports: Assistance by persons without disabilities to a person with a disability within a work or leisure settings.

Receptive language: The process of receiving and understanding spoken or written language, or gestures.

Self advocacy: To speak for oneself or to have someone else speak in the behalf of the person with a disability in order to make choices and decisions.

Sheltered workshop: A work setting in which employee with a disability participates in contract work, usually on a piece-rate basis, such as preparing bulk mailings or refinishing furniture.

Supplemental Security Income (SSI): A federal program administered through the Social security Administration that provides payments to individuals who are elderly or have disabilities. Children may be eligible for SSI if they have disabilities and are from families with low income. In addition, children who are hospitalized for 30 days or more and have a disability expected to last 12 months or more may receive SSI.

Supported employment: Paid employment for a worker with a disability in settings with people who are nondisabled. A job coach provides support to the individual with a disability by helping the individual improve job skills, interpersonal relations, or any other job related needs.

Transition: The process of moving from one situation to another. Frequently used to mean moving from school to work and the community.

Transition planning: Careful preparation by the student, parents, educators, and other service providers, for the time when the student leaves high school. The plan is written in the Individualized Transition Plan.

Transition services: A coordinated set of activities for a student that promotes movement from school to post-school activities, including post secondary education vocational training integrated employment continuing and adult education adult services independent living or community participation.

Work activity centers: Programs for adults with disabilities, providing training in vocational skills, as well as daily living skills, social skills, and recreational skills.

Resources to Explore
Community Living Information

Magazines and Newsletters

The Advocate.
The Autism Society of America,
7910 Woodmont Avenue,
Suite 300,
Bethesda, MD 20814-3015
(800) 3AUTISM ext. 150
(301) 657-0869 (fax)
E-mail: action_alert@autism-society.org
Wed: http://www.autism-society.org.

The ARC
The Arc of the United States

1010 Wayne Avenue
Suite 650
Siver Spring, MD 20910
(301) 565-3842
(301) 565-5342 (fax)
E-mail info@thearc.org
Web: http://www.thearc.org

Autism Asperger's Digest
Future Horizons, Inc.
721 West Abram Street
Arlington, TX 76103
(800) 489-0727

Autism Research Review International
Autism Research Institute
4182 Adams Avenue
San Diego, CA 92116
(619) 281-7165
(619) 563-6840 (fax)
Web: http://www.autism.com/ari

Exceptional Parent
Psy-Ed Corp
555 Kinderkamack Road
Oradell, NJ 07649-1517
(877) 372-7368
E-mail: Webmaster@eparrent.com
Web: http://www.eparent.com

Inclusion News. Centre for Integrated Education & Community
24 Thome Crescent,
Toronto, Ontario M6H2S5
Canada

Journal of Autism and Developmental Disorders.
Kluwer Academic/Plenum Publishers
233 Spring Street
New York, NY 10013-1578
(212) 620-8468
(212) 807 1047 (fax)
E-mail: services @wkap.nl
Web: http://www.wkap.nl/journalhome.htm/

Looking Up: The Monthly International Autism Newsletter
P.O. Box 25727
London, SW19 1WF England
(181) 542-7702
E-mail: LookingUp@compuserve.com
Web: http://www.feinst.deon.co.uk/looking-up.html.

MAAP Newsletter.
More Able Autistic Persons, Inc.
P.O. Box 524
Crown point, IN 46307
(219) 662-1311
E-mail: chart@netnitco.nt
Web: http://ww2/netnitco.net/users/chart/maap.html

The Morning News.
Jenison Public School
Editor: Carol Gray
2140 Bauer Road
Jenison, MI 49428
(616) 457-8955
(616) 457-4070 (fax)
E-mail: edfuture@onramp.net
Web: http://www.futurehorizons-autism.com

News Digest, Parent Guides, and Basics for parents.
NICHCY
P.O. Box 1492
Washington, DC 20013
(800) 695- 0285
E-mail: nichcy@aed.org
Web: http://www.nichcy.org

Organizations

Autism Research Institute
4182 Adams Avenue
San Diego, CA 92116
(619) 281-7165
(619) 563-6840 (fax)
Web: http://http://www.autism.com/ari/

Autism Society of America
7910 Woodmont Avenue
Suite 300
Bethesda, MD 20814
(800) 3-AUTISM
(301) 657-0881
(301) 657- 0869 (fax)
Web: www.autism-society.org

Division TEACCH
CB#7180
310 Medical school Wing E
The University of North Carolina at Chapel Hill
Chapel Hill, NC 27599-7180
(919) 966-2174
(919) 966-4127 (fax)
E-mail: teach@unc.edu
Web: http://www.unc.edu/depts/teacch/

The Doug Flutie, Jr. Foundation for Autism
C/o The Giving Back Fund
54 Canal Street
Suite 320
Boston, MA 02114
(617) 556-2820
(617) 973-9463 (fax)
E-mail: giveback@ma.ultlranet.com

The Indiana Resource Center for Autism
Institute for the Study of Developmental Disabilities
Indiana University
2853 East Tenth Street
Bloomington, IN 47408-26601
(812) 855-6508
(812) 855-9630 (fax)
(812) 855-9396 (TTY)
E-mail prattc@indiana.edu
Web: http:// www.iidc.indiana.edu/~irca/

National Information Center for children and Youth with
Disabilities (NICHCY)
P.O. Box 1492
Washington, DC 20013-1492
(800) 695-0285
(202) 884-8200
(202) 884-8441 (fax)
E-mail: nichcy@aed.org
Web: http://www.nichcy.org

TASH (formerly the Association for Persons with Severe
Handicaps)
29 W. Susquehanna Avenue
Suite 210

Baltimore, MD 21204
(410) 828-8274
(410) 828-6706
E-mail: nweiss@tash.org
Web: http://www.tash.org/

Internet Resources

Autism Network International
Web: http://www.ani.ac

Autism Resources
Web: http://autism-info.com/

Disability Resources Monthly
Web: http://www.disabilityresources.org

National Institutes of mental Health (NIMH)
Web: http://www.nimh.nih.gov/publcat/autism.cfm

Employment and Transition Planning and Housing
HEATH Resource Center
National Clearinghouse on Postsecondary Education for
Individuals with Disabilities
Suite 800 One DuPont Circle
Washington, DC 20036
(800) 544-3284
http://www.health-resource-center.org

Respite
ARCH National Respite Locator
Service and Resource Center
Chapel Hill Training Outreach Project
800 Eastowne Drive

Suite 105
Chapel, Hill, NC 27514
(800) 7RELIEF (773-5433)
http://www.chtop.coom/locator/html

Books

Dileo, Dale. It's My Meeting! A Family/Consumer Pocket Guide to Participating in Person - Centered Planning Meetings. St. Augustine: Training Resource Network, Inc., 1996.

Smith, M.D., Belcher, R.G., and Juhrs, P.D. A Guide to Successful Employment for Individuals with Autism. Paul H. Brookes, 1995.

Suomi, J., Ruble, L. and Dalrymple N. Let Community Employment Be The Goal for Individuals with Autism. Bloomington: Indiana Resource Center for Autism, Indiana University, 1992.

Bibliography

Advocate. Autism Society of America. (2001, July).

Hayden, M.F., and Abery, B.H. Challenges for a Service System in Transition. Ensuring Quality Community Experiences for Persons with Developmental Disabilities. Baltimore: Pal H. Brookes, 1994.

Mount, Beth, Beeman, Pat, and Ducharme, George. What Are We Learning about Circles of Support? A Collection of Tools, Ideas, and Reflections on Building and Facilitating Circles of Support. Manchester, CT: Communitas, 1988.

Suomi, J., Ruble, L. and Dalrymple N. Let Community Employment Be The Goal for Individuals with Autism. Bloomington: Indiana Resource Center for Autism, Indiana University, 1992.

Shapiro, J.P. No pity: People with Disabilities Forging A New Civil Rights Movement. New York: Times Books, 1993.

Smith, M.D., Belcher, R.G., and Juhrs, P.D. A Guide to Successful Employment for Individuals with Autism. Paul H. Brookes, 1995.

Wing, Lorna, *The Austistic Spectrum. A Parent's Guide to Understanding and Helping Your Child.* Berkley, CA: Ulysses Press, 2001.